SAI MUSINGS
ANECDOTES OF A SAI BABA DEVOTEE

SAI MUSINGS
ANECDOTES OF A SAI BABA DEVOTEE

KABITA MOHANTY

STERLING

STERLING PUBLISHERS (P) LTD.
Regd. Office: A1/256 Safdarjung Enclave, New Delhi-110029.
Cin: U22110DL1964PTC211907
Mobile: +91 82877 98380/+91 120-6251823
e-mail: mail@sterlingpublishers.in
www.sterlingpublishers.in

Sai Musings: Anecdotes of a Sai Baba Devotee
© 2021, Kabita Mohanty
ISBN 978 81 950824 5 2

All rights are reserved.
No part of this publication may be reproduced, stored in a retrieval system or transmitted, in any form or by any means, mechanical, photocopying, recording or otherwise, without prior written permission of the original publisher.

Printed and Published in India by

Sterling Publishers Pvt. Ltd.,
Plot No. 13, Ecotech-III, Greater Noida - 201306, U. P. India

Prof. Ganeshi Lal
Governor, Odihsa

RAJBHAVAN
BHUBANESHWAR - 751008

MESSAGE

April 16, 2021

I am glad to know that 'Sai Musings' authored by Kabita Mohanty and published by Sterling Publishers is being released on the auspicious day of Akshaya Trutiya, 2021.

Smt. Kabita Mohanty is a banker by profession and a writer by passion. Her earlier book *'Eka Akchanara Anubhuti'* has been well received and the English version of this book 'Sai Musings' is meant for greater readership. Her writings are highly popular among Sai devotees. May Sree Sai Baba bless her with more success in future in all her endeavours.

I congratulate the author and wish the publication all success.

(Ganeshi Lal)

Tel : 91-674-2536111/2536222, Fax : 91-674-2536582, E-mail : govodisha@nic.in, Website : www.rajbhavanodisha.gov.in

NAVEEN PATNAIK
CHIEF MINISTER ODISHA

LOKASEVA BHAVAN
BHUBANESHWAR

MESSAGE

I am glad to know that Kabita Mohanty of Bhubanswer is releasing her devotional book 'Sai Musings' on the auspicious day of Akshaya Trutiya 2021.

Published by 'Sterling Publishers, this book is the English version of her Odia Book *'Eka Akinchanara Anubhati'*. Both the versions are a divine treat for the devotees of Sai Baba. In a world of materialism, divine experience brings solace to the soul. Only the blessed ones experience these sacred moments of life. The book has all the fragrance of divinity.

I congratulate the author and wish the publication a great success.

(NAVEEN PATNAIK)

PRASANNA K PATASANI FORMER MEMBER OF LOKSABHA

MESSAGE

'Sai Musings' written by one of the recognized poet and writer of our state Kabita Mohanty is the pride of our state Odisha. Her name is named by her parents as poetry. Her spontaneous overflow of divine feelings do influence us. This is possible only because she could reach higher state of consciousness, in other words zero state of mind which I tell it as unified field. By the blessings of Baba ,she got absolute consciousness, always feels the presence of Baba in and around her. To me, it is one type of deep divine realisation within which bestowed upon her by Sai Baba which is reflected not only in her articles or poems but also the present book 'Sai Musings'. The reading of the book, I am sure will leave an indelible print in the minds of Sai Devotees and all other readers. I am delighted and amazed after going through chapter wise stories of the book reflecting her divine experience. Her articles in the book penetrate to the heart and soul with vibration to attain blissful state of consciousness.

I wish her more and more writings by the blessings of unseen divine power of Lord Sai Baba which will bring peace and prosperity to the society.

Joy Shree Sai.

(PRASANNA KUMAR PATASANI)

Blessings from Guruji Dr. C.B. Satpathy

'Sai Musings', the anecdotes of Shirdi Sai Baba written by Mrs. Kabita Mohanty, is the English version of her Odia book 'Eka Akinchanara Anubhuti'. The Odia book is highly appreciated by Sai devotees of Odisha. Mrs. Mohanty is AGM in UCO Bank and presently working under Ministry of Financial Services as DGM on deputation. From the manuscript, it is clear that she went to Shirdi in 2008 for the first time but she had experienced the presence of Baba much earlier. This book is based on her sheer love and devotion for Baba. Every story depicts how she feels the presence of Baba in her day-to-day life. She, along with her husband, visited Shirdi many times and visited all the places which are close to Baba.

She had met me at Tankapani Sai Mandir in Bhubaneshwar and at Sai ka Aangan in Gurugram as described in the book. She not only visits different Sai temples but also follows the path of wisdom preached by Sai Baba. In every small happening in her life, she felt the presence of Baba – whether the idol of Baba came to her house suddenly or she participated in palki yatra. The feelings of different devotees may not always be same, but there are some similarities always. Shri Dabholkar also compiled the divine experiences of different devotees in 'Shri Sai Satcharita'.

This book is written in a lucid and simple language which will touch any reader, besides Sai followers. The divine deeds and preachings of Shirdi Sai Baba cast their magic spell all over the globe. During the last two decades, the stream of Sai Movement in the state of Odisha has been accelerated. Thousands of devotees from Odisha are visiting Shirdi to receive the blessings of Sai Baba. At this point of time, I strongly feel that this book will be very useful to all Sai followers and other readers. It will inspire others, too, to write on Sai Baba.

I sincerely pray to Baba to bless Mrs. Mohanty to write more and more such types of books which bring solace to humankind.

Dr. Chandra Bhanu Satpathy
Gurugram

Preface

Just a few years ago, I was asking, 'Who is this Baba? Do these miracles really happen to these people?' And when I started following Him, I would frequently ask myself when I would also go through the miracles of Shirdi Sai Baba experienced by other devotees about which I read in different magazines. Without my knowledge, I got attracted to Baba with every passing day. I don't remember when He started occupying the position of the seniormost member of our family. Yes, He came, I saw, He conquered.

It's over two decades since I first visited the Sai Temple at Tankapani Road, Bhubaneswar, in 1999. Then I got engrossed in my personal and professional life. For some time, Baba took the backseat. Only His innocent, calm and composed look flashed in my mind and disturbed me time and again. Slowly, He pulled me into His blissful world. Every now and then I experienced some miracle by His divine blessings. It is not I alone, but millions of Sai followers experience such miracles regularly. But for me, it was as if He told me to write down all those miraculous experiences as His messenger. Due to a variety of reasons, I couldn't write about all my blissful experiences until 2011 when I joined as a faculty in the UCO Bank Training College at Bhubaneswar.

Preface

It is He who arranged my posting at Training college, Bhubaneswar. I would steal some time to write down my experiences whenever I got a gap between sessions. Many of them were published in different Sai magazines in Odisha. Then a silent call came within to publish all those unspoken stories which I had experienced over the years. Miraculously, He arranged my transfer to Delhi on a deputation post to CERSAI under Ministry of Financial Services, Government of India. That was not the end of the story. Being away from home, a hollow feeling formed within me. Suddenly, the stream of poetic thoughts running through my blood became a stream of lava from a volcano and I went on composing poems after poems. In a year, I wrote almost two hundred poems. They were published in different magazines and newspapers in Odisha.

My family advised me to compile together all the poems which were appreciated profusely by the readers. But my wish was to publish my experiences with Baba as the first book. Then only would I go for the poem compilation. These are all His leelas which is beyond my imagination. Both books, *Eka Akinchanara Anubhuti* (prose) and *Sahara Samparka* (poems) in Odia were released on the same day at a Sai temple on 8 September 2018. When many Sai devotees said that it was a good act to publish the books during the centenary year of Shirdi Sai Baba, I didn't have any answer to that.

Did I really do anything? Or as I used to say, an Old Man sitting in my balcony or near the window listens to my unspoken words, my innermost desires and the next day the same get materialized. Yes, it's true that all pure desires are always fulfilled. On the day of the release of the book, I was advised by a few friends and readers to publish an English version as well. It was again His call to start the English translation through His messengers. Rev. Guruji C.B. Satapathyji's blessings in the Odia book inspired me to start the translation.

Just three days after the Odia book release, on 11 September 2018, I started translating. My family encouraged me a lot to go ahead with the translation work. My younger son Ishan did a good job by refining the English and typing the whole manuscript in book form. While doing the work, he wished that the book was published by Sterling Publishers and my immediate reply was that we should do our work, the rest Baba will do. Yes, Baba again listened to our conversation and we contacted Sterling Publishers, whose Managing Director, Mr. S.K. Ghai, smilingly agreed to publish the book and gave it to his most experienced editor, Mr. Sanjiv Sarin to edit.

Much water has flown under the bridge during these two years. The pandemic virtually took away 2020, but my wish to see my baby *Sai Musings* before 31 May, the day of my retirement, is again fulfilled by the Old Man, my Baba, listening from the balcony.

It is beyond human abilities to understand the leelas of Sai Baba. One of His 11 sayings is, *'I shall be active and vigorous even after leaving the body and my tomb shall speak for the welfare of the devotees.'* This is true for all Sai devotees. As Baba said, He will take everything He wants from the devotees in His own way. Maybe, I am blessed to do this part of writing by Baba's direction. My pen won't stop, my talks won't end when they are related to Baba.

I am always in a trance, though I am in the cobweb of worldly life.

And for me, this is never an end but the beginning of *Sai Musings!*

Contents

	Preface	x
1.	The Maiden Touch	1
2.	Griha Pravesh	5
3.	A Ladoo a Day Keeps the Doctor Away	9
4.	I Am Because You Are	13
5.	Going Bananas	19
6.	The Road Not Taken	23
7.	Circles of Faith	28
8.	I'm Possible	32
9.	Finding Joy in the City of Joy	35
10.	The Whitening Effect	38
11.	Change Is Not the Only Constant	41
12.	Floodgates	45
13.	Behind the Scenes	49
14.	Round the Clock	53
15.	Only the Believer Knows Where the Ant Bites	58
16.	Ma'am You're Next	62
17.	The Voice from the Other Side	66
18.	Patience or Belief	69
19.	A Strike for Good	72
20.	Booked for Life	76
21.	Omniscient	79

22. Omnipresent	81
23. Eternalized Mortal	84
24. Counting on Hope	86
25. Throwback Thursday	90
26. Essence Matters and Not Appearance	94
27. Never Wished but Always Granted	98
28. A Known Mystery	104
29. Down but Not Out	109
30. The Forbidden Fruit	113
31. Faith Healing	118
32. Serendipity	123
33. Lost and Found	127
34. The Missing Crown	132
35. You Have One Unread Message	136
36. Happy New Year	140
37. Service Before Self	144
38. Last-In First-Out	149
39. Sai-Chology	153
40. The Light at the End of the Tunnel	158
41. Ring a Bell	163
42. The First Invitee and the Last in Attendance	170
43. Loop of Devotion	174
44. A New Beginning	176

1

The Maiden Touch

The first experience about anything in life is always unforgettable – the first day in school, the first bicycle ride or the first love of your life. Likewise, the first miracle of Shirdi Sai Baba I experienced shall be a memory of a lifetime.

It goes back to the late 1990s in Bhubaneswar, Odisha. The first Sai temple in the city was under construction at Tankapani Road. My dear friend Smita Panda and her husband, Suresh Panda (or Suresh Babu as he was usually called), both ardent devotees of Sai Baba, were blessed to undertake this divine work. Smita and I have been friends since college days. Though we had the same subjects and were in the same class, I was indifferent to her devotion towards Sai Baba. Her convent schooling, impeccable smartness, modern outlook, broad mindedness and humane values ensured she always remained grounded. I both admired, and bonded well with her. We have remained in touch through all possible means that have evolved over time, be it landlines then or cellphones now and, at times, platonic telepathy – maybe because of Baba's invisible and invincible holy blessings.

Smita was completely involved in the construction of the Sai Baba temple. She used to talk about Baba over phone and I enjoyed listening to her. Often, I wondered how this girl, schooled in English medium, was speaking at length about Sai Baba in pure Odia language. Each time I asked her 'Who is this Baba?' she asked me to come and visit the temple. Finally, the Staapana (installation) of the idol of Sai Baba took place. After that, she used to enlighten me about a few religious practices undertaken at Sai Baba temples, for example, Pran Pratistha, Abhishek, Mahasnana and others, followed by a fervent request to visit the temple and have a darshan. Though my preoccupations did not allow me to visit the temple, I seemed to be seeing and drawn close to Him through Smita's phone calls. Smita then became a lecturer in a college and I joined a reputed bank – UCO Bank.

Coincidence plays a definite role in everyone's life. One day, Smita, my dear friend who had been my companion all this while, was on the other side of the bank counter enquiring whether I, as an employee of UCO Bank, could help her in opening a Trust Account of Tankapani Sai Mandir. In spite of being a junior employee, I gathered courage to go and ask my senior, who turned down the proposal. That event left my first attempt to work for Sai Baba unsuccessful, leaving me down but not out.

A few days later Smita told me about a monthly magazine *Sai Bani*, an assimilation of experiences of various Sai devotees, which was published on behalf of Tankapani Sai Mandir. Knowing my interest for reading, she advised me to get a copy and without much ado, I opted for an yearly subscription. Even until that day, I had never been to a Sai Baba Mandir.

The first copy of *Sai Bani* reached me through a person deputed by Smita who handed me my copy and collected the subscription amount at my bank itself. I continued

The Maiden Touch

receiving the copies for two years, until Suresh Babu got transferred from Odisha. His transfer brought about an abrupt end to my subscription. That familiar face stopped turning up at the bank with my copy of *Sai Bani*. Those pages in the magazine were not just some personal experiences of devotees but provided a sense of equanimity and growing belief for me. I used to look forward to the magazine every month like a child waiting for the father to return home from work.

Once, my lovely, septuagenarian mother came to my house at Bhubaneswar and saw the magazines. While reading them, she started developing an attachment to Sai Baba. She took all the copies of the magazines and asked me to send her the future ones too. But I couldn't do that since my own subscription had stopped.

Things seemed gloomy for a few days. Then suddenly Smita called me and rekindled my hope for reviving the subscription. It felt like the experience of the first shower after a long drought. She gave the name of the person at the Mandir to whom I should send the subscription. I requested my husband to take me to Tankapani Road, but he was very busy and couldn't help me. For a couple of days, a feeling of helplessness and despair took over me. But then, suddenly there was light at the end of the tunnel.

I can clearly recollect the day when I was at the bank counter, busy attending customers, but mentally thinking of ways to reach the temple and get a copy of *Sai Bani*. Out of the blue appeared Mr. Hemant Mishra, a colleague who had been transferred to another branch in the same city. He said, 'Madam give me ₹60, I have paid for your magazine,' referring to *Sai Bani*. For a moment, I was dumbfounded. All I could hear was 'I have paid for your magazine.' I had not spoken to Mr. Mishra for two years, ever since he had been transferred from our branch. So how could he pay for my subscription? Hence I politely enquired how he knew that my subscription was due. He said that he had gone to the temple for darshan when an office bearer of the temple management met him. The well-spirited official knew that Mr. Mishra worked in UCO Bank. He said that there was a lady Kabita Mohanty in UCO Bank who subscribed to *Sai Bani* but hadn't paid the subscription and hence was not receiving the magazines. Without a second thought or seeking a confirmation from me, Mr. Mishra paid the amount to renew the subscription. And now he sought the refund from me.

Mr. Mishra's words were simple and crisp, devoid of any sense of wonder or excitement which otherwise was so palpable in me. For him it was a simple, obvious thing to do. His words flew across the counter and left me speechless and dumbfounded. The words, 'I have paid for your magazine' made a huge impact that day and still resonate in my mind today.

The chain of events can be called as a mere coincidence, but from the perspective of a devotee, when an event emerges out of the impossible, the believer acknowledges by bowing down with obeisance and says out aloud 'Sai Ram'!

2

Griha Pravesh

My elder son Lt. Cdr. Koushik Kanungo, serving in INS Karanja, Mumbai, had successfully graduated and completed the daunting course of the National Defence Academy (NDA) in 2007, which filled us all with pride. We had sent a boy to Rashtriya Indian Military College (RIMC), Dehradun but when he stepped on the Antim Pag (The Final Step) at NDA, Pune, we saw a gentleman emerging.

Before going to his Passing Out Parade (POP) I had a word with a family whose ward was also an NDA alumnus, who had visited Shirdi, Trimbakeshwar, etc., after his POP. A strong desire to do that and then relax and refresh at Goa took over my husband and me. When my younger son, Ishan, lovingly called Chintu, and elder son Koushik, lovingly called Guddu, came to know about our plan, they wanted to join in as well. Everything was fine, but after the POP, Guddu had to obtain several clearances from different departments before he could leave NDA, thus delaying our plans. The boys suggested that my husband and I should continue with our Shirdi programme and meet them at Mumbai airport directly. We were not keen on leaving two young boys on their own and did not agree to their proposal. I accepted the fact that maybe Sai

Baba's call hadn't come yet. Or rather, Guddu's clearance protocol stalled my call!

The following year Guddu was posted at Lonavala and invited us to visit him at his base. I said yes, with the condition that I would go to Shirdi first. He agreed and booked the tickets for our to-and-fro journey. Somehow, the confirmation of the return journey was pending till the day before our date of travel. Anxiety had gripped me and I debated whether to cancel our train tickets and fly to Mumbai instead. I was in a state of complete confusion when my dear friend Smita called. Before listening to why she had called, I just went on sharing my issues of the Shirdi trip. She had a hearty laugh and said that I should have called her earlier for the ticket confirmation. I could not understand how she could help till she said she was working in the Tourism Department at New Delhi and could easily manage the confirmations.

We reached Mumbai and then left for Shirdi in an overnight bus. Amidst all this confusion, I forgot to take my medicines for blood-pressure and gastric ailments, resulting in severe vomiting during the bus journey and I felt very exhausted. My body was very weak due to the severe vomiting. Somehow, my husband and I checked into our hotel which was at a stone's throw distance from the temple.

I lay on the bed and all my plans – which saree to wear, how will my meeting be with Baba, will it be worth all the distance trudged, etc., seemed to relay in front of my eyes. With all these thoughts in mind, I felt sleepy. I did not have strength to get up and get ready for the Baba's darshan. My husband coaxed me to get ready saying that this trip would be a waste otherwise. Physically and mentally tired, I somehow got up and stood in the long line for the darshan. I did complete the darshan but not to my satisfaction, without all the childlike bubbling energy and excitement that had filled me up earlier.

Griha Pravesh

After darshan, we were wandering in the temple compound aimlessly when my husband suggested that we should purchase a few idols before leaving Shirdi. I walked into a shop but didn't purchase anything. Meanwhile, Guddu had been calling incessantly but our phones were lying in our hotel room. His eagerness to see us had now changed into concern which was confirmed when he heard my sickly and shaky voice over the phone. He and my husband decided that we should leave Shirdi and join him immediately. Since bumpy bus rides caused me nausea, he said we should take a cab for Lonavala without any delay.

Something like this had happened to me for the first time and I just couldn't understand why. Travelling outstation was an annual ritual for us and getting some antiques or souvenirs as a memento was a standard practice. But this time I returned empty handed from Shirdi, even though I had been keen to purchase some idols. I can't understand the reason even now, though I have contemplated every possible cause. Nevertheless, I was happy meeting my son. I distributed the prasad to him and his colleagues and, after a brief stay, we came back home. I kept brooding over the reason for not buying any idols, be it while cooking or during lunch-breaks at office with colleagues. The thought stayed with me all the time.

An octogenarian pensioner, Mr. R.N. Mohanty, was one of our customers. I had always attended him with utmost care and respect and met his service requirements diligently. Due to my warm approach and deft handling of his queries and requests, he would address me as his daughter, which used to tug at my heartstrings. Handling the customer was my job but handling him well was a pleasure. Five days after I returned from Shirdi, he called and requested my colleague who answered the phone to connect him to his daughter, i.e., me. He asked me to send someone to his house, which was nearby, because he had something for me.

When my messenger returned, I was flabbergasted. I couldn't believe my eyes. My desk was overflowing with Sai Baba – there was a Sai Baba idol, a Sai calendar, Udi, incense sticks, pendant with Sai Baba's picture, ladoo prasad and so on. Overjoyed, tears started streaming down my face. My messenger said that both Mr. and Mrs. Mohanty had been to Shirdi and got all this for me. I rushed to my dear colleague Jayshree, who's less a colleague and more a friend, and asked her to have a look at my desk. Jayshree knew all about my Shirdi visit, my sudden sickness and my lack of satisfaction with the trip.

When I had walked into the shop at Shirdi for purchasing an idol, I had enquired from the shopkeeper about a particular idol which I had liked. Exactly the same idol was now sitting at my office desk. Overwhelmed at seeing me cry in joy, Jayshree said, 'Madam, Baba came to you because you were searching for Him in your mind.' My rational self could not understand that. I asked her, how was this possible? Calmly she said, 'Madam, you're blessed because He has come to you all by Himself. Everything happens by His direction only.'

Baba hasn't let anyone come empty-handed from His doors. He blesses everyone who devotes themselves to Him, irrespective of gains or losses, grief or pleasure, success or failure. When I delved deeper into His world with my 'why', He opened the door for me and stood at the threshold. He entered my home just like what in the age-old tradition is called 'Grih Pravesh'.

3

A Ladoo a Day Keeps the Doctor Away

When health is lost, something is lost.

I had seen this once in my elder son's moral science book. This thought haunted me throughout the harrowing experience I had with some gastro related health issues in 2008-2009.

More than the fear of being diagnosed with something which seemed daunting to overcome initially, it was the ensuing mental pressure that affected my spirits. My concentration at work was weakened, my mental composure was disturbed and invariably it was my family members, more particularly my husband, a lawyer by profession, who had been affected the most. My husband couldn't hide his tension, no matter how hard he tried. A fear of the unknown gripped me and mental fatigue took over. All the usual diagnostic tests like ultrasound, endoscopy and colonoscopy were performed. I also completed the course of medicines prescribed by Dr. Dalei, a gastroenterologist of high repute in Odisha, without satisfactory result. He then advised me to undergo a capsule endoscopy at Visakhapatnam, since it was not available in Odisha, to identify the root cause of the problem. I was quite an active person and used to go regularly for a morning walk. I also followed a balanced diet. So my question was, 'God, why me?' This question 'Why me, Baba?' came rushing to me frequently.

Meanwhile my elder sister, Mrs. Kalpana Mohanty, whom I called 'Apa' (she called me 'Pachi'), a retired headmistress, called to ask our well-being. Apa had been a fervent and devout devotee of Sai Baba since a long time. Her penchant for academic books had resulted in her having read profoundly about Baba as well. Though I had seen Baba's immaculately framed photo in her pooja room, I was not aware of this fact.

She arrived at our place just after the phone call. She had come alone and it was around 9 p.m., which by Bhubaneswar standards was not a safe time to travel. So she was in a hurry to go back. She had come all this way just to advise me to perform the Pancha Guruvar Brata, which involved observing and performing a ritual and a fast on five consecutive Thursdays. Though she didn't carry any book describing the ritualistic pooja, she hurriedly explained it to me verbally. She also said that Baba did not believe in performance of the ritual by following everything exactly as prescribed. A clean heart and a clear conscience were more essential than anything else. She also advised me to continue the prescribed medicines and not to discontinue them.

I had placed Baba's idol in the house in one of the alcoves in the staircase. The primary reason for such an unusual placement was to be able to see Him when I left home. The following day was a Thursday, so I decided to implement what Apa had advised and accordingly Baba found His due place in my pooja room. I also started the Pancha Guruvar Brata.

The first thing I could perceive and feel after performing this ritual was a clear change in the atmosphere prevalent in and around my home. All of a sudden, a sense of equanimity seemed to have pervaded every corner of my

A Ladoo a Day Keeps the Doctor Away

home. An unidentified yet soothing scent seemed to waft in and around the pooja room. Was it the incense sticks or was it something indescribable? Though the medical reports were the same, I felt a change in myself. At times, I used to walk into the pooja room just for the peace it gave me.

Apa had also made a mention of doing Narayan Seva after the completion of Pancha Guruvar Brata. I wanted to do this at the Sai Mandir at Tankapani Road, but the temple was too far away. Meanwhile, a few of my colleagues who were to perform this ritual suggested that I join them in distributing some light refreshments outside the temple. But I declined, because I had made a commitment to myself that I'd do this at my choice and time, and for my own satisfaction.

In the meantime, I was posted as the branch head at Balianta Branch, which was almost at the periphery of Bhubaneswar. This was the mandatory rural posting. What seemed challenging in terms of distance seemed to bring hope and blessings as the Sai Mandir at Tankapani Road was on the way to the branch.

As an employee of the bank, I was entitled to a lumpsum amount every year of ₹5,000 towards medical expenses. It was the first day of 2010 when both money and goodluck got credited into my life again, leaving me indebted towards Him. I could also now follow my Apa's advice of performing the Narayan Seva with this amount.

It was the morning of 2 January 2010 when I alighted from my two-wheeler in front of the Mandir. That day, not being a Thursday, didn't have the usual crowd of devotees, lost to the world, in a religious trance, so I could park my two-wheeler right in front of the temple, between the trees, without any difficulty. I went in after removing my shoes. I completed my usual darshan, had tirth (holy water) and went to the temple office to pay for my annual dhoop deep and prasad for Baba. Then I walked to the parking lot and was slipping my feet into my shoes when I felt something soft inside them. I bent down to have a look and to my utter shock I found it was a ladoo, neatly wrapped in paper inside the shoe.

I looked around for a beggar who may have kept it and then looked upwards towards the tree in case a bird had dropped it, but found nothing. By that time my watch was announcing 'late to office', so I kept the ladoo in my bag and left. Questions about the identity of who had kept it filled me the whole day. In the evening, after I reached home, I replaced my office bag with a new one, forgetting all about the ladoo.

The next day, while I was chatting with Mr. Panda, a colleague, I told him about the ladoo I had found. He immediately responded, 'Madam, you observed the Pancha Guruvar Brata and completed the Narayan Seva but you couldn't understand that the ladoo was His blessing for you? You should eat it and you will be cured of your gastro ailments.'

Before I could get carried away by what he said, I remembered the doctor's advice, 'One of the causes of the stomach problem is some bacterial infection which might be from unkempt nails, dirty hands or unhygienic foods.' What if the ladoo was dirty? I kept wondering about it till I got back home. I immediately took out the old bag, forgot all about the doctor's advice and with absolute faith in Him, I ate all of the ladoo, till the last bit.

They say doctors are the physical manifestation of God. Well, the reverse is also true. Neither did the need to go to Visakhapatnam for capsule endoscopy ever arise after that, nor did the pathology reports detect anything after that.

4

I Am Because You Are

With every passing day I was getting to know Baba more and more, but I wanted to delve still deeper. My involvement with Him grew manifold. My entire life seemed to be governed by Him. In fact at one point I realized He had become the centre point of every activity in my life. I called Apa to discuss this growing attachment. She suggested I should perform Sai Parayan, which can be done according to my convenience – in a day or two or a fortnight or one chapter a day. She said she had recently completed it in a single day, which awakened the spirit in me and I thought, 'If she can, why can't I?' My spirit and devotion for Him wanted me to start immediately, but my resolution to perform Sai Parayan somehow couldn't be fulfilled due to my responsibilities at home and office. But Baba always finds His own way.

At that time, Guddu, my elder son, was posted at the Naval Academy, Kochi, for his pre-commissioning training. One day, out of the blue, he called up at the bank to tell me that he had docked at Vizag and had couple of days of leave. Since Vizag was so near Bhubaneswar, he was eager to meet us and would come home. My happiness and joy were cut short abruptly when he telephoned after a while to say that he did not get permission for going out-of-station during his leave. He sounded very dejected. I immediately asked if he could meet me if I came over instead, and he said yes. I called my husband, who was at a friend's place, but owing to prior commitments, he said he couldn't go with me. He booked my tickets and my zonal manager sanctioned me a two-day leave saying 'Family comes first.'

Then Guddu called again to say that he was coming home the next day as his leave was finally sanctioned and asked me to keep his arrival secret, as a surprise to his father. I called my husband again and requested him to cancel my tickets, making up some flimsy excuse.

While returning home from the bank that evening, I was feeling happy with anticipation of meeting my son soon, but fate had other plans. At home, when I tried feigning ignorance about Guddu's visit, my husband cut short my remarks saying that Guddu wasn't coming home as his leave permission had been withdrawn. Guddu couldn't inform me directly as I hadn't answered my mobile. It was in my bag and I didn't hear it ring. So he had called his father instead. I was obviously disheartened and rang Guddu. He was feeling sad, too. He said his seniors had torpedoed his visit due to some sudden change in training schedule.

That night in bed, tears came streaming down at the thought of being deprived of seeing my son. My restlessness didn't allow me to sleep and I kept regretting cancelling my tickets in haste.

The events took a toll on me the next day, which was a Wednesday. Though I had been granted a two-day leave, I was still in office. My colleagues were surprised to find me there. Seeing my sad face, they avoided asking me anything. Absentmindedly I looked at the calendar and realized that the next day was a Thursday – Baba's day!

Suddenly an idea occurred to me that I could perform Sai Parayan in one day. Without much ado, I left office at midday and requested my office folks that I would be on leave the next day and not to phone me. I told them that I'd disclose everything on Friday.

The thought of doing Sai Parayan in one day lifted my mind from the despondency I felt. In the afternoon I made all arrangements like cleaning the pooja room and getting all the ingredients for prasad. The task of selecting a picture of Baba took time. I had an assortment of pictures which adorned every nook-and-corner of my house. Finally, I chose a picture which didn't have the contemporary style of the modern-day portraits. It was a small, red coloured portrait which hung in the balcony. Every morning when I sat in the balcony, in that picture it seemed as if He was looking at me. Moreover, this first sight of Him every morning augured a brighter start to my day.

At the crack of dawn, I was in the pooja room with the holy Shri Sai Satcharita to fulfil my commitment and His call. My husband had left town for some work by the time I was about to start my rituals. So that day at home it was just Baba, I and my recitation of Shri Sai Satcharita. I didn't eat a morsel the whole day as I had vowed to finish the book by the evening. I didn't take any breaks except for tea as it works as a stimulant and energy booster for me.

I vividly remember I completed reading Shri Sai Satcharita at 7.32 p.m. and called my husband to share the news. He has a religious bent of mind and suggested augmenting the day's virtue by visiting the Sai Mandir at Tankapani Road. The long distance and eeriness of the dark and deserted by-lanes leading to the Mandir didn't deter me. So, I prepared some suji halwa prasad and left for the temple. My spontaneous decision and courage to take my two-wheeler didn't stem from any rational logic. I felt brave and adventurous like an NDA cadet doing the undoable.

I reached the temple safely and had completed my pooja when I met Mrs. Panda, my friend Smita's mother and an ardent devotee of Baba, who is also a Mandir Trustee. Out of love and respect I call her Mausi. In my excitement and joy, I happily shared with her about my one-day Sai Parayan. She enquired repeatedly about the reason behind it – whether I had any wish to be fulfilled. I told her it was a mere coincidence and shared the story of Guddu's leave and my impromptu decision.

Out of care and concern, she asked me if my husband was with me as it was late and this was the closing time of the temple. When I continued my narration, she again enquired my mode of conveyance. Meanwhile Smita's father, or Mausa ji as I called him, who had overheard our conversation from the office room, came over and said, 'Kabita, it is already late, almost 10 p.m., and the road is lonely. You should leave immediately.' I answered him with the casualness of a relaxed Thursday evening, saying, 'Mausa ji, these days I'm not feeling afraid as I feel there is someone with me round the clock.' He offered me some khiri (kheer) prasad and suggested again to leave quickly.

It was 10.30 p.m. when I reached home. Just before entering the gate, I called out to Bapi to offer prasad and share the one-day parayan story. Bapi was in his late teens and stayed in a shed adjacent to our house. He did petty tasks as a manual labourer for his living. But most importantly, he was an ardent devotee of Sai Baba and never failed to visit the temple in spite of his destitution. He was a frequent visitor to our house. With our common devotion towards Sai Baba, he was my 'Man Thursday'. When he came over, I narrated him the day's events and asked him to come and feel the fragrance of Baba's presence in my pooja room. But he continued standing at the doorstep, unmoved and still like a rock. His reaction was not at all what I expected.

After a while he said, 'Maa, I want to say something. Rather I have some bad news.' His ominous tone got me worried, but I tried to keep calm and said, 'You can share with me.' He said, 'Maa, last night I had a nightmare where I saw your death and a sea of wailing people in and around this building. I was mentally disturbed a lot and I told my mother about it. I was even more taken aback and shocked when I didn't see you at the balcony this morning and then Sai Baba's photo was missing from your balcony wall. I have been looking for you since morning and praying my dream was not true.'

I replied, 'Oh! That is why I was doing Sai Parayan the whole day in that pooja room.' I smiled and asked him to come and see Baba first. He came behind me to the pooja room, offered his prayers and I gave him some prasad. Once he left, I came back upstairs. But the strangeness of his dream started to affect me since I was completely alone that day. The fear in me was increasing and so I decided to speak to Apa, even though it was so late.

I narrated the whole story up to that moment to Apa. She thought about it and then said, 'Pachi, Baba is behind you, warding off evil that tried hovering over you and your family by making you immerse yourself in Him. He impeded your movements by confining you within those four walls of your pooja room by making you perform Sai Parayan.'

I understood what Apa was saying. From Guddu's permission for a short leave being withdrawn at the eleventh hour to cancellation of my tickets in haste, from my sudden decision to perform the Sai Parayan in a single day without any prior wish to Bapi's foreboding dream – I joined the dots. Apa's voice broke my reverie when she said, 'People wish for the outcome before sitting for Sai Parayan, whereas you got everything without asking for it.'

The moment Apa hung up, the loneliness I had been feeling gave way to the realization that He was with me all the time. Tears welled up, along with a smile that kept widening. I dozed off to a sound sleep with one of His hymns playing in my mind.

In His world of belief and faith, the end is never a possibility and possibilities never end. From His perspective, every end is a new beginning.

5

Going Bananas

Because some things are nothing but Baba's leelas.

My devotion towards Baba was continuously on a rise. It was not out of fear or need of favour, but love and only love for Baba. I read in many stories and hear several people say that Baba's favourite prasads are bananas and misri or rock candy. I had cultivated a small house-garden with coconut, mango, guava and most importantly banana trees, and secretly nurtured a wish to give Baba my home-grown bananas.

The sleepy Sunday afternoon didn't tempt me with the pleasures of my comfortable bed. I fought the temptation valiantly and took a stroll in the backyard of my house, when I reached the banana plantations. Their sight reminded me of my desire to offer Baba prasad of my home-grown bananas the following Thursday. But all the bananas were too raw to consume. Nature came in the way of my sincere devotion. The next week I made it through my office and work from the exhausting Monday to the exhilarating Wednesday. What Friday evening is to the youth, Wednesday evening is to me. Friday evenings tend to be the start of the weekend party for today's generation and for me the air of Wednesday wafts with a fervour and freshness of Baba's Thursday. I returned home from work on Wednesday evening, freshened up and walked over to my balcony to relax over a cup of tea. Before I could even sit down, I saw a wonderous sight. Just to be doubly sure, I rushed forward to check. I wasn't disappointed. One of the banana trees, which had a branch stretching to the roof of my adjacent outhouse, had yielded to my secretly nurtured wish. The bunch of bananas it had were perfectly ripe, fit for an offering, with a few ripe ones having already fallen on the roof. Happily, I plucked a bunch and offered them to Baba the next day, His Thursday.

During my stint at the Balianta Branch, paying obeisance to Baba at Tankapani Mandir had become a daily ritual during my to-and-fro journey to office. I offered Him the home-grown bananas whenever I could. In the everyday race that makes life fun, I tend to have a race with my husband every morning – who leaves home first for office. The one left behind has to lock the house and lose out several minutes and seconds, so crucial to reaching office on time. Each tick of the second hand of the wall clock sounds like 'get set–go'.

The previous evening I had kept a handful of bananas packed, on the sideboard near the main door, to be picked up while leaving for office, for my usual offering. I got ready quickly the next morning and rushed downstairs to leave for work on my two-wheeler when I felt a little dizzy and nauseous.

Having been diagnosed with blood pressure in 2005, I keep the timings of my medicines regular lest it causes any untoward incident. I avoid missing them inadvertently by keeping a few doses in my bag so that if I miss taking them at home, I can have them after reaching office. I stooped near my porch with my head reeling and realized that I hadn't had my morning dose. Once I got grip of myself, I knocked on the door of the tenant who was staying downstairs and asked her to give me a glass of water. I put my hand into my bag for my pills when I suddenly smiled to myself. My husband, who had lost the race that day, stood by the door giving me company, worried about my well-being and seemed to question my sanity when he saw me smile for no reason. When I had opened my bag, I found my pills but not the bananas that I had planned to offer Baba that day at the temple and realization dawned on me.

I rushed upstairs to get the bananas and came back with a pleased smile on my face. My worried husband and the concerned tenant were taken aback by the sudden change in me – from feeling sick to smiling. But I stayed quiet, lest my explanation diluted the divine flavour of my experience. The inadvertent missing of my medicine was indeed a gentle reminder in the subtlest way.

It was in late 2014 when I was deputed to my present organization, the Department of Financial Services, Government of India at New Delhi. Every summer and winter vacations became a family reunion for me. My husband would fly down from Bhubaneswar, and Guddu and my beautiful daughter-in-law Luis would come from wherever they were posted to join my younger son Chintu and me.

Each time my husband came, he brought along with him an assortment of home-grown vegetables and fruits, thanks to the caretaker who ensured a neat and secure package for it to survive the cargo handlers of the airlines. That vacation when my husband came with the usual box, I immediately opened it to have a feel and effervescence of home and home-grown produce. The first thing I saw were three bunches of unripe bananas. The same old wish resurfaced at the sight of the bananas, but they would take time to ripen. I packed them carefully and kept them at a conspicuous place at the storeroom.

The ensuing madness, the air filled with laughter, tables covered with empty cups from the endless bouts of tea drinking and the melodious voices at my home diverted my thoughts away from the wish I had nurtured and the bananas remained in the storeroom.

The next day I had a hectic day at the office. When I came back home, I was tired and dozed off after saying hello to everyone at home. It was 3 a.m. when I suddenly woke up, all restless and impatient, and with the words from my dream still repeating in my head, 'Hello! Hello! Wake up!! Have you forgotten about the bananas? They have ripened!' Bewildered due to the voice that shook me from my sleep, I ran to the storeroom to check. Realization dawned on me when I opened the packet containing the bananas and found fully ripe ones waiting to be taken out and offered to Baba. The interesting thing was that my husband had arrived on Saturday evening and the bananas had ripened at unusually superfast speed by Wednesday night, ready to be offered on Thursday, or rather, Baba's day.

I will wrap up this story with some food for thought. Not everything in the world is the result of human actions. Not everything in the world has the backing of scientific evidence, logic or reasoning because some things are nothing but Baba's leela and His divine play.

6

The Road Not Taken

Given a choice, people always choose the obvious and known road and not the unconventional or unknown one because security always has an upper hand over uncertainty.

Promotions and transfers are a common feature of most jobs. They are the steps of the ladder of growth. I had served diligently at the Government Secretariat Branch from 2006 to 2009 when the grapevine was abuzz with the news of a rural posting for me as a Branch Head, which was the normal progression in my career. All my colleagues who were in the queue to be elevated to Branch Heads had been pulling every possible string and lobbying hard for a comfortable posting. But I was mentally prepared to accept whatever came my way, agreeing with my husband's philosophy – never impede the natural process of any event because there is always a hidden lesson.

Near the national highway, there was a branch situated at a place called Janla, which was where the Zonal office intended to post me. So my colleagues started calling me 'Branch Manager, Janla', to which I simply smiled. This kind of humorous leg-pulling is never left behind at school or college but transcends time and reaches our office, too.

The orders were to be issued by the end of the day, and there was a general commotion in our office in addition to the usual queries and requests from our customers. While Janla posting seemed to be fixed for me since long, suddenly I had a strong urge to prefer a posting at Balianta (Balakati area) Branch. This was another rural branch located at the opposite end of the road to the Janla Branch. Both were around 10–15 km from my house. Even till today I do not know why and how this thought of opting for a posting at the Balakati Branch germinated. But the feeling was so strong that I decided to call my ex-boss, who was earlier heading the Secretariat Branch (which handled the postings) and was then posted at Assam. I avoided any small talk after the customary greetings and straightway expressed my desire to join Balakati Branch and requested his help. He concurred with my choice and said that the road to Janla Branch was unsafe for women to commute by two-wheelers and Balakati was comparatively better.

Within the next five minutes my fate was decided when I received a call from the Zonal Office asking me, 'Madam, Janla or Balakati?' I immediately said 'Balakati'. Before I could ask who it was at the other end, the person put down the phone. It seemed as if a genie had called to grant me my wish.

I returned home and was busy with the usual household work when I got a call from a senior colleague who said, 'Congratulations!' When I enquired the reason, he replied, 'Aren't you aware that you've been posted as Branch Head at Balakati Branch? Anyway, tomorrow there is a meeting at Zonal Office, Bhubaneswar and you should be present.' I was so excited and overwhelmed on receiving the news that I forgot to thank the caller.

Though the next day was Sunday, a weekly off, the Zonal Office was teeming with all the new Branch Managers. A few people congratulated me but also cautioned that

Balakati Branch was in a state of turmoil and faced several problems. They enquired whether I had done any background check before opting for it, but my reason was different and had nothing to do with the wafting gossips.

The following day, 27 July 2009, holds much significance for me not only because I was entrusted with the Herculean responsibility of handling the branch, but also because my husband had dropped me at office for the first time ever. The excitement of finally being on the other side of the desk and doing best what I'd done over decades was amplified when I entered the Manager's cabin. Just opposite the manager's chair was a beautifully framed photo of Baba! While I was taken aback by His surprising yet welcome presence there, I heard Baba saying, 'Welcome! Welcome!'

Being the first woman to take over as a Branch Head amongst all other nationalized and private banks in the area had created ripples in those days. The agricultural town was full of this news, my support staff told me. Suddenly everyone, from the land-tillers to the land owners, started visiting my cabin. While the tillers talked of their hardships and problems, the owners tried to make their importance felt from the start itself – the usual societal hierarchy! Nevertheless, shying away from work and responsibility was not my character, so I started from basics and tended to the numerous problems and complaints, with patience and perseverance.

During many one-to-one interactions, a few customers expressed apprehension about my commuting route to the bank on my two-wheeler, through the main road. Gradually the numbers of good Samaritans seemed to increase and their concern changed into advice for changing the route. I was oblivious to all this till Mr. Sahoo, a customer who had become a familiar face owing to his frequent visits as a cash-credit account holder, gave me a sensible and prudent reason. He said that the main road was risky as it was overflowing with traffic, especially of trucks and buses, but if I took the alternate route, I would face less traffic and the distance was also a kilometre less. When I enquired the alternate route, he said that from Bomikhal to Rabi Talkies Square, I should take the road by the canal, then turn left to reach Tankapani Sai Mandir and then take the connecting bridge over the river to reach the bank. He appeared quite familiar with the route, so I asked a few clarifications. But his mention of Tankapani Sai Mandir– the place from where the sapling of my devotion grew – stayed in my mind.

There was a female colleague, an assistant manager, who had been posted in my branch since the last two years. She also commuted via the main road using a two-wheeler. I asked her whether she had ever been advised about the alternate route. She said that it was lonely and deserted route, with the bare minimum lighting. Even in the afternoons, it was rare to find a single soul there, leave alone in the evening. I was caught in a dilemma of either being reasonably sensible or devotionally blind. In case of a problem, the main road teeming with people and vehicles might be a better bet than the isolated road, where I would only have the Invisibly Invincible, my Baba.

The very next day I took to the second route, rather 'the road not taken', and stopped in front of the Sai Mandir for a while. Though I didn't alight from my two-wheeler, I bowed in subservience before Him and raised my hands acknowledging his guiding presence and then hurriedly drove by the bridge to my branch, because biometric attendance doesn't acknowledge devotion.

Taking the route to the office via the temple earned me the guidance and presence of Baba, just like the North Star showing the direction for travellers to reach their destination, He became my guide for life and beyond. The series of events, right from the rumours of Janla posting, to

The Road Not Taken

the voice on the telephone that asked me to choose between Janla and Balakati within a moment, from the sea people who came to seek a solution for their banking problems but ended up showing me care and concern for me, to the clear suggestion of Mr. Sahoo where the most suitable road was via Baba's temple, all seemed to fall into place.

The unquenched longing to visit and see Baba was satisfied when seeing and being with Him became a daily routine, both in the morning and the evening. As mentioned in the holy Sai Satcharita, Baba can pull a flying bird with a string as if its legs are tied with it. Whether He bound me or was I captivated by His omnipresence, I was always filled by His presence.

7

Circles of Faith

Devotion, if limited by fear or favour, doesn't yield satisfaction to the heart. Rather, it becomes a transactional act where we pray and in return want Him to grant our wish. Gains, whether tangible or intangible, material or intellectual, have always been important in the endless list of human wants. It's only if we separate gains from devotion, that things automatically fall into place for our betterment because Baba can see through us clearly.

As mentioned earlier, I was blessed to have darshan of Baba at Tankapani Sai Mandir every day. Sometimes I visited Baba even three times a day – whenever I could manage a few minutes during lunch time, in addition to my morning and evening visits. The ensuing satisfaction and happiness can neither be quantified nor expressed in mere words – some things are just meant to be felt. Love and devotion for Him are two of them.

During one of my visits, I had finished paying my obeisance to Baba at the Gurusthan when I saw a pile of books about Him kept there. Devotees often formed long queues to get a copy. I followed suit. I was lucky enough to get one. At home I started reading it to see His world through the perspective of another follower. Any new

Circles of Faith

activity often tends to spike up the interest levels initially, before other mundane priorities seep in to dilute its novelty. The habit of reading a few pages before retiring somehow got diluted in the exhaustion of my daily to-and-fro office commute, and household and office work.

One Wednesday, I happened to check the bookmark to see the number of pages I had read. To my utter disappointment, I had barely managed 50. The idiosyncrasies of childhood refuse to go with age. They somehow continue as one's existence and personality. Having been an ardent reader since my school days, I used to read the last chapters when I felt bored in the middle of the book. So that night before sleeping, I repeated my quirky habit and read the last chapter.

That Thursday, or rather Baba's day, I was more enthusiastic to go and pay homage to Baba at the Tankapani Sai Mandir. While returning from office, I went to have darshan. On my way back to my two-wheeler, I saw a group of devotees gathered before the parayan hall. On enquiring, a bystander told me, 'Maa, this is the Sai Palki which is being readied for the Chawadi jatra. This is a ritual that is done here every Thursday. Are you not aware of this?' Before I could respond, my eyes caught the picture of Baba placed on the Sai Palki and I stood in awe of the radiance He transmitted. He seemed to illuminate the darkness in our lives with the brilliance of His eyes. I admired how delicately the devotees decorated the Sai Palki. The dexterity of their hands reflected the innate love and respect for Baba. After every minute detail was checked, the Sai Palki was finally lifted on the shoulders by the devotees to complete the sacred five rounds. The grandeur of the Palki elicited the spontaneous chants of the devotees. In the backdrop of the lighted alley and illuminated Sai Palki, the periodic rising of hands by the devotees in reverence formed a silhouette of subservience to the Master Himself. The crowd's excitement gradually increased because each devotee wanted a chance to shoulder the Palki. While some tried elbowing their way forward, other broke down during the chants and prayers. Those tears were a sign of reverence and devotion towards Him. I too was a part of the frenzied crowd, mesmerized by the innocence of His eyes, with tears streaming down my cheeks, hands clapping in time with the hundreds of others, and following the Palki to complete the five rounds of faith.

Meanwhile, during all this, I had totally forgotten to keep a track of the time and the transition of the crimson hued evening to the pitch-dark night. It was almost as if I had passed through impermeable time and had been restored to my senses only upon completion of the Chawadi jatra. My happiness and sense of fulfilment were jolted when I saw couple of missed calls from Guddu and an unknown number. My heartbeats increased because so many missed calls automatically give rise to fear and apprehension when your son is serving in the defence forces, and especially when he is undergoing arduous trainings. With trembling hands I dialled Guddu. His ever chirpy and lively voice slow and filled with pain. My equanimity went for a toss upon hearing him. I became so nervous that I even found it hard to ask anything. Guddu, at the other end of the phone line, started speaking slowly stopping intermittently. He was playing cricket when the ball bounced from an uneven portion of the pitch and struck him in the face. I was frantic with worry. No mother can bear the pain her child undergoes. Tears of reverence now changed into endless streams of tears of apprehension. His inability to speak clearly made me worry more. Then a coursemate took the phone from Guddu and told me, quite level headedly that Guddu's condition wasn't alarming. It was just a cut on his cheek, below his eyes. If it had been an inch higher, it would have been a problem, but Guddu had a narrow escape and was recuperating well after his wound was stitched at the military hospital. His words calmed me a

Circles of Faith

little. He added that there was nothing to worry as several of the coursemates were present with Guddu round the clock to look after him. I turned around and looked at the enormous structure of the temple and thanked the omnipresent Baba. I raised my hands in respect to thank Him for protecting my son from danger.

When I reached home I got busy with the usual household work. While cooking, I started thinking where had I recently come across the Chawadi jatra and Sai Palki. Then I remembered. The previous night, the last chapter of the book to which I had jumped, had a detailed description about Chawadi jatra and Sai Palki. That night, as I read the chapter again, with each sentence, I could hear the drum beats and passionate chants of the hundreds of devotees carrying the Palki on their shoulders. I was teleported into state of Sai trance where I could picturize myself in the sea of unknown faces held together by the bond of Sai and being a part of the Chawadi jatra. I had a feeling of immense calmness. I wondered if I could ever get a chance to put my shoulders to the Sai Palki.

While I was immersed in the sea of devotion that day and was a part of the momentous procession, Baba protected my son against an imminent threat. He protected Guddu and my pradhakhina in His Chawadi jatra remained unhindered. I got much more than I sought. A small desire to carry His Palki got fulfilled and Guddu escaped safely, if not unscathed. The gravity of my problems was lessened, and the happiness of my fulfilment was doubled.

Did I ask less, or did He give more? Whatever He gives outweighs our wants. Pray, not transact. Worship, not ask.

8

I'm Possible

Rituals cannot be imprisoned within the confines of a religious rulebook, else Baba would belong to a class and not the mass. In other words, capturing the essence of one's faith and belief through performing rituals with the available means and resources is what gives an individual satisfaction and brings him or her closer to Baba.

As mentioned earlier in 'A Ladoo a Day Keeps the Doctor Away', it was during the difficult times in 2008, when I was diagnosed with gastro related issues, that my elder sister, Apa, had come over to my house to tell me how to perform the Pancha Guruvar Brata, that is, to and perform certain rituals on five consecutive Thursdays. I vividly recollect she told me the basic ingredients needed to do the pooja were a green coconut with a shoot (shoot is called 'laasi' in Odia), a piece of red sieve cloth (called 'saalu kanaa' in Odia) to wrap the coconut, sandalwood paste, vermillion and flowers, along with Baba's idol or photo. Additionally, as offering, banana and misri were used. Amidst all the listed items, the image of a green coconut with a shoot wrapped in a piece of red sieve cloth somehow etched itself permanently in my mind. I believed that it was the basic requirement for performing the ritual.

I'm Possible

I still remember keeping the coconut wrapped in the red sieve cloth on a brass kalash with water inside.

This pooja became a regular activity for me every Thursday resulting in an air of positivity pervading in and around my home. But most importantly, it took my mind off the health issues that had marred my spirits. So, with renewed vigour and energy, I vowed to make this Pancha Guruvar Brata into a weekly ritual every Thursday. That was easier said than done because though zeal and enthusiasm steered me through the first five or six weeks, demands of work and home prevented me from continuing. Nevertheless, this ritual stuck to me though it became an intermittent affair over the years.

A startling incident occurred in the month of February 2010. One Wednesday we had to attend a marriage reception at Paradeep port. Since it was at a considerable distance from Bhubaneswar, my husband and I started early. During our return journey, I suddenly realized that I didn't have even the most basic pooja item – a coconut with a shoot – to do the pooja the next day, a Thursday. I was restless and had a disturbed sleep that night. When I woke up early morning, I decided to buy a coconut with a shoot from the shops near my house. I went there quickly but to my utter dismay the shops were closed. There is always a gain in a loss, because I'd have burned some extra calories that day even though I returned home empty handed. Office time was nearing, so listlessly I purchased a dry coconut from a general store nearby. I feared that the pooja would be incomplete without a coconut with a shoot – just a dry coconut may not count in the merit of the pooja. I realized I was speaking my thoughts loud enough to make passers-by give me stares as if I was weird or had lost my mental balance.

When I was going upstairs to my house, I kept muttering to myself that my pooja would be incomplete without a green coconut while my husband and domestic help were standing near the staircase, smiling at me. Before I could ask the reason, my husband asked me whether I had noticed anything in the garden while leaving the house in the morning, to which I said no. Actually, when we had constructed this house in 1992, we had planted two coconut trees inside our compound in front of our building which had grown to a great height over the years. When my husband was taking his morning walk, the domestic help arrived and said she had seen two coconuts lying on the ground at that early hour. The strange thing was that out of the two, while one was dry, the other was an unripe, green one. It is natural for dry coconuts to fall automatically but a green one falling is a rarity.

That day the pooja was to my satisfaction and my wish was fulfilled. This incident of a green coconut falling in the early hours of the morning of the same Thursday when I needed it urgently for my pooja which I couldn't get anywhere, created another milestone in my spiritual journey. While driving to office, I tried to find the reason for the event, yet could only smile to myself with a contented heart, for I was wholly and solely devoted to the one I nested my faith in – Baba.

A glass looks half-full or half-empty, depending up the thoughts and vision of the person. Likewise, rationality would have searched the crutches of reason and logic to find the exact cause behind the mysterious fall of the coconut, but devotion and faith in Baba would make you believe that only He can make *impossible* look as *i'm possible*.

9

Finding Joy in the City of Joy

It was during mid-2010 when I was selected for a week-long training at UCO Bank Training Centre, Salt Lake, Kolkata. I don't believe in blowing my own trumpet but being the only lady amongst the chosen and highly efficient 30 Branch Heads did make me swell with pride. Hard-work and sincerity always yields results over time, provided you have the key of patience and perseverance.

After the enriching yet exhausting training on the first day, I took a walk around Salt Lake with a thought of finding Baba somewhere. I did find a Shiv Mandir, if not Baba's. Maintaining my belief, I made it a point to visit the Shiv Mandir every day just to savour the peacefulness and serenity which pervaded the atmosphere there. The training programme ended on a professional high and we all departed to our respective branches to continue with our jobs, with fresh learnings.

Almost a year later, around September, I was back at the same place for another training and was lucky enough to find the company of some fine female colleagues that time. Wolves hunt in packs whereas women shop in packs. So, the three of us often went around the city during the weekend for shopping, walking into every shop along the lanes we were traversing. All my colleagues got themselves something or the other according to their choice and pockets. My heart was on a beautiful dress in an unusual shop which caught my attention while I was walking. Within a moment I decided that I would use it as a dress for Baba's idol kept at my home in Bhubaneswar. Without a second thought I purchased it.

Back in our rooms, we were discussing about our shopping extravaganza when I mentioned my small yet meaningful purchase. The discussion slowly drifted towards Baba and His miracles. We talked late into the night before we finally went to sleep. The following day was a Wednesday and having been an early riser all my life, I woke up and went for a stroll. I walked to the same Shiv Mandir that I had visited during my previous visit. I finished my usual pooja and turned around to leave, when I saw an amazing sight. Near the boundary of the temple several idols of different gods and goddesses were kept – Vishnu, Ganesha, Hanuman, etc. Amidst all of them I found the familiar face, with the same constant gaze – my Baba. I remembered that my earlier visit, though enriching from a professional point of view, still left some emptiness inside when I couldn't find Baba during several walks in and around Salt Lake.

Before I could immerse myself in the overwhelming sea of happiness, I noticed something unusual. While all the other idols there were impeccably dressed, Baba was not. Luckily, the dress I had purchased the day before would fit him well, I realized. I proposed to the priest that I would give the dress the next day, which was a Thursday – Baba's day. Happily, he agreed. On Thursday, I also offered a garland to add to His pure grandeur. Paraphrasing from Sai Satcharita, the essence of which was captured before me – *He takes away the things in whatever way or from wherever, if it is due from someone.*

Finding Joy in the City of Joy

I had a coveted chance again for training in the same Salt Lake training institute after six months or so. Going to that Shiv Mandir was no more a leisurely excursion like the first time but more like being drawn to Him like a bird on a string. When I had visited the temple in the morning I winced at the sight of a dull and grubby Baba's idol with a prominent crack on the side. Immediately, I asked the priest if there was any shop nearby from where I could purchase a new idol to replace it. He said that it would be available at Ganesh Ghat, which was quite far from Salt Lake. Since I could not travel all that distance, I offered a decent amount to the priest with a feverish request to get a new idol. He assured me he would get it by the evening that day, which coincidentally was a Wednesday. The next day was Thursday – Baba's day. I couldn't contain the happiness and satisfaction I experienced when the following morning the priest did the sacred Abhishek Pooja and installed the idol. This might not be significant for a person who hasn't been a part of His world, but for a devotee these things are not just invaluable but reinvigorate their instilled belief in His holy existence. Otherwise, I could never have been a part of this sacred ceremony of installation of Baba's idol in a temple which was far away from my home – in the City of Joy.

10

The Whitening Effect

Keeping the child within you alive is the key to your rejuvenation at any point of time. Having had a childhood amidst the extravagance of nature in a rural area, my knack for nurturing and caring for plants was natural and gardening had always been my cherished pastime. I also loved making garlands with the flowers when I was young as much as quickly devouring ripe mangoes before any of my siblings had a chance.

My husband has been an active member of the Rotary club since a long time and played a key role in the rise of regional Rotary clubs in Bhubaneswar. As a result, we get a chance to attend several conferences in and around India.

The Rotary conference in Sri Lanka took place from 11 to 16 November 2010. Sri Lanka is a beautiful place. Surrounded by the Indian Ocean, the whole country is a photographer's delight and on every global traveller's wish list. Watching the peaceful blue sea running parallel to the tarmac road, a person is sure to drift deeper and deeper into serenity. While going around the city in our tourist buses, we saw white crepe jasmines ('tagara' in Odia) everywhere along the roadsides. The shrubs were so flush with flowers that their whiteness covered green leaves. The sight was so endearing that for a brief moment I felt like requesting the bus to halt so that I could pluck a few. I silently imagined making a garland out of these flowers and offering it to a deity in white – which by default had to be Baba. Buddhism was the predominant religion there, so Lord Buddha's temples dotted every part of the island nation. Ironically, the colour of Lord Buddha's idols was often an impeccable white.

The small yet significant wish of preparing a garland from white crepe jasmines and offering it to Baba seemed to cast its spell on me. It was so embedded in my head that on the night preceding our return journey, I dreamt of the same thought manifesting itself in real life. When I looked at the clock, it was early morning, and folklore and age-old belief is that dreams seen in the morning always come true.

The relaxing trip came to an end but my dream remained. I returned to my city and to work also. On 17 November we proceeded to Chandrashekharpur, a well-developed high-rise area in Bhubaneswar, to check the status of our second house which was under construction then. In fact the ground floor had been ready since 2004 but the second-floor construction had picked pace only in the last few months. I had planted a crepe jasmine plant right in front of the gate way back in 2004. The plant did bear flowers, but not in abundance. The quantity it bore acknowledged its presence but didn't cater to the religious needs of a home.

Upon reaching there, while my husband went into the building to check the new fittings and woodwork, I was awestruck and couldn't believe what I saw. The sight was a treat for me just like a cone with scoops of vanilla ice-cream is for a child. The plant was full of white crepe jasmines and a whole bunch was already strewn on the ground. Without losing any time, I requested my driver to get a carry bag, while I frantically tried to collect as many flowers as I could.

The following day was a weekend. I was oblivious to numerous requests for tea from my husband, or the workload at the bank and sat down in my balcony with the sun rays falling on the flowers kept in front of me on a newspaper. With each bunch of crepe jasmine passing through the needle, the thickness of the garland increased and I got closer to fulfilling my wish.

I remembered the dream I had seen in Sri Lanka. I felt as if the rays from the sun were the rays of hope, with the message to never let go of dreams. They will become true sooner or later. Thankfully, it was sooner in my case.

11

Change Is Not the Only Constant

During my stint as a Branch Head at Balakati Branch, I frequented Shirdi Sai Baba Temple on Tankapani road at least twice a day as it was situated midway on my route to office. These visits became a part of my daily routine – like breathing is to existence. My visits went up to three times on days when I had a meeting at the Zonal Office, which was at Bhubaneswar. The exhaustion of driving a two-wheeler under the scorching sun was eased at the thought of getting a chance to see Baba yet again. His sight had the same effect as finding an oasis in a desert.

During one of my regular visits to the temple, I went to the Gurusthan and when I saw the small yet spotlessly white marble idol of Baba, I deliberated upon offering a hand-stitched dress to Him rather than a readymade one. I enquired from the priest who frankly told me that the dress received from the devotees was donned by Baba only once as they received numerous such offerings and everyone should get a fair chance. Fair enough! All are equal before Him. I went ahead with my idea, purchased a cream-coloured cloth and stitched it with glittering gold brocade around the border. I clearly remember it was a

Monday, sometime in February 2010, when I offered the hand stitched dress at Gurusthan. The moment the dress was put on Baba, I was transfixed at the sight. The soothing colour accentuated the tranquillity of the white idol of Baba. For some time, I was glued to His silent and serene gaze over the radiance of the handmade dress. While returning from office that day, I visited the Gurusthan again to have a glimpse of Baba and just couldn't take my eyes off Him. For me it was more than a dress made up of satin; it was a fabric of unadulterated love bordered with brocades of undying affection and stitched with the threads of devotion.

Having been a frequent visitor, I had become familiar with some people not through introduction or befriending them but by being tied with the same invisible thread of love that all of us have for Baba. One such young person, Happy, visited the temple daily and would sit silently in a corner and look at Baba. That day at Gurusthan I saw Happy savouring the sight of Baba in the new dress. I went up to him and told him that the dress that Baba was wearing was stitched by me. He replied, 'Maa, Baba looks adorable in this dress.' Appreciation from kith and kin is obligatory, but from a third person it is not only genuine but also a big morale booster. Hearing those kind words of appreciation, I was overcome with unbridled joy. But I also remembered the words of the priest – dresses received from the devotees are donned by Baba only once. I stood still and kept admiring the idol which was radiating good vibrations, filling the atmosphere with positivity. The day finally came to an end but not the flow of His omnipresent aura.

In March, around Holi, my younger son Ishan, or Chintu, came home on a short leave from his law school. The day before Holi, which is a Poornima, is my birthday as per Hindu calendar. After dinner, both of us were chatting and eventually the talk drifted to Baba and His miracles. He is a boy of a few words and a keen sense of observation like

Change Is Not the Only Constant

every introvert, I assume. He was describing how he had managed to get a ceramic tile to place the idol of Baba at an elevated position in his hostel room. I had given him this idol when he had joined law school. He said he used to light incense sticks daily before leaving for his classes. When he returned from class the air was filled with an aroma which was not just the perfume from the incense sticks but something undefinable yet significant. Small things add to affection. That he had done this filled me with pride and motherly love.

I told him about the hand-stitched dress that I presented to Baba. I tried painting a picture before him on the canvas of fond memories with the colours of sheer devotion. He suddenly stood up and asked whether he could see the dress that I had offered to Baba. I told him that Baba wore a dress only once. But we decided to visit the temple the following morning anyway, even though I knew that Baba would be donning the fabric of another devotee's love and affection.

Chintu is usually a late sleeper, but that day he was up early in the morning. Both of us set off for the temple. The entire journey was performed in silence. Maybe our silence was conspiring something for us. Upon reaching the temple, I told Chintu to get two diyas from the nearby shops while I proceeded towards Gurusthan.

When I reached there, I couldn't believe my eyes and stood transfixed. That moment I felt as if Baba was waiting for me to acknowledge His supremacy yet again. I walked towards Him, bowed in obeisance and touched His dress to check what I had seen and to raise the bar of devotion towards Him. This was the same cream-coloured dress, with the gold brocade I had stitched! The touch of the fabric shook me to the core and left me in a state of daze. The next thought that came to my mind was to fetch my son Chintu. Hearing my loud call, he ran towards the Gurusthan with the diyas in his hand. He too was amazed and asked, 'How is it possible that Baba is wearing that dress again? You said every dress is worn by him only once.'

I was equally dazed and confused as my son. Baba and only Baba can change the rules and laws. He had even changed the rule followed in the temple.

Just like His world is not limited by boundaries, His miracles don't have an expiry date, because for the next four consecutive Mondays, Baba donned the same cream-coloured dress. On my way to the bank and back, I was surprised about this each time. Just to reconfirm, I would touch the dress and feel the fine golden brocades. At the end, it was Happy who provided the answer to this miracle. He said, 'Maa, perhaps Baba loves your hand-stitched dress so much that He has been wearing it repeatedly for the last few Mondays.' All I could respond was, 'Maybe.' It seemed Happy, the familiar stranger, had been observing the miracle, too. The end of logic, the reversal of science and the interruption of standard practices is nothing but the threshold of the gateway that leads to Baba's unending world of miracles.

12

Floodgates

Having spent my childhood in a rural area, I enjoy gardening and the fruits of my own efforts, be it vegetables for the kitchen or a bunch of flowers for the Deity. Even when I moved to the city for greener pastures, I never forgot my roots. This reflected in other walks of my life like cooking, bringing up my children or stitching a dress for Baba.

My elder son Lt. Cdr. Koushik, or Guddu, celebrates his birthday on 4 September. Somehow the idea of offering a dress to Baba on Guddu's birthday came to my mind. Despite the responsibilities of being a Branch Manager on my shoulders, I didn't let my resolve weaken. A fortnight before his birthday, I went to Padma General Store at Bapuji Nagar, a shopping area in Bhubaneswar, where you can find almost all kinds of fabrics at a reasonable price. The moment I stepped in, I saw a shade of cloth on the upper racks which, as per my recollection, had never been donned by Baba that year. It was a hue of purple whose magnificence can't be described in mere words and it etches itself into the memory of the viewer. I was excited about finding something so beautiful and purchased it immediately.

I stitched the dress with all the finesse and love for Baba and handed it to the office of Tankapani Road Mandir two days before Guddu's birthday. From the time I had purchased the cloth, I was full of the excitement, wishing to see Baba in that dress. Expecting appreciation, I requested my eldest sister Apa and her husband, who stayed nearby, and a colleague-cum-friend, Jayashree, to go to the temple on 4th September to have a look at the dress. I was on leave that day as I wanted to perform a pooja at home. I had also collected Tulsi leaves for preparing a garland for Baba to wear when He would be decked in the dress I had lovingly stitched for Him.

I went to the temple early morning with my husband and a friend, Pushpanjali. Expecting to being flooded by a sea of compliments for my choice of the dress, I finished my rituals. But to my utter shock and dismay, I barely heard a word of praise from anyone. The feeling of disappointment was clearly visible on my face. I left the temple with a sad heart as neither my husband nor my friend had any word of appreciation for me. My soul felt like a hungry child looking for smallest morsel of anything edible to quell the hunger.

I kept waiting for calls from Apa and my friends whom I had informed about the dress. But no phone call came. Out of desperation and as a last measure, I rang up my friends, but with no result. None of them could make it to the temple that day.

I got busy with my daily routine and completely forgot the incident. Three days later, on 7 September, which was a Saturday – a respite for any banker as it is a half-day for work. On my way back from office, I visited Apa and then both of us went to Tankapani Sai Baba Mandir for making arrangements for a Seva. While walking towards the office, just in front of Parayana Hall, I saw two ladies approaching from the opposite side. One of them asked me, 'Are you

Floodgates

Kabita Mohanty?' I expected her next statement would be for some help for bank related work. But surprisingly, she started praising the dress I had offered on Guddu's birthday. She praised the magnificence and the uniqueness of the colour. She said Baba hadn't looked more beautiful throughout the year as He looked that day.

Her words of praise were music for my ears and a balm for my soul. That unknown lady seemed to be like a messenger of Baba to rejuvenate and rekindle my faith in Him. She continued asking me questions about where I had got the cloth from, whether I had stitched it myself or got it done by a tailor, etc. I was overwhelmed and tears welled up. Her words opened the floodgates of my emotions. Oblivious to everything, I started crying uncontrollably like a child, with the people around staring at me in amazement.

In my emotional state, I heard the lady (Sanchita Rath, as I came to know later) continue talking about the special dress that she had seen. Her friend said that the colour was so unique that it can't be described in mere words, one had to see it to appreciate its magnificence. For the last three days they had been visiting the temple with the hope of finding the person who had offered the dress. The priest had directed them to the office. One of the office bearers told them that the dress was offered by one bank madam who was a frequent visitor to the temple. Sanchita Ma'am was so besotted with the dress, that she wanted to purchase it when it would be offered for sale to the devotees.

Eventually my uncontrollable crying stopped and I regained my composure. Happy with her praise and with a large smile on my face, I answered all her questions.

After coming home, I sat down in my balcony. The soothing evening breeze brought the events of the afternoon to my mind again. Reviewing them, I realized that Baba had put my patience to test and then sent a beloved messenger, who was not known to me, yet was bound by the love for Him, who showered me with adulations which sounded like the thoughts I had in me when I walked into that store in Bapuji Nagar to purchase that cloth. His test put my expectations to simmer till its optimum level on the furnace of patience and then He sent a beloved messenger to develop my love and devotion for Baba, like never before.

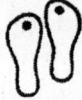

13

Behind the Scenes

Nami muttered under her breath, 'How is Baba helping you when you keep chanting His name all the time? Why didn't He come to your help at this odd hour?'

Buying gold on days like Akshaya Tritiya and Dhanteras is considered as auspicious. The purpose of such purchases is to make Lakshmi Maa stay in our house to provide prosperity and bestow wealth. Thus, losing gold has always been considered as a bad omen and owing to my humble rural beginnings, such old beliefs are deeply ingrained in me.

In 2010, my husband, Kailash Kanungo, became the Chartered President of the Rotary Club Confluence, Bhubaneswar. He had been associated with that club since long and had been involved in all the philanthropic activities that aimed at serving the society. The Club used to convene their meetings at the prestigious Hotel Crown. One Sunday a grand Club event was arranged. I decided to help my husband instead of just going for the event. As always, he was busy making the entire arrangements. Having bought a mangalsutra recently and not being able to use it till then, I thought of wearing it instead of my regular gold chain. I hurriedly put the mangalsutra in my bag and went downstairs. I locked the door and kept the bunch of keys in my bag, sat in the car and instructed the driver to drive to Hotel Crown. In the car, I took off the gold chain I was wearing, kept it in my bag and put on the mangalsutra. At the event, I mixed with the crowd and had a good time with friends.

Suddenly I got a call from Nami, the girl from my village who used to come to help in the house whenever I asked her. She would help in daily household work like stitching, gardening, etc., while I listened patiently to her griefs. Nami said that she was waiting outside our residence. I told her I would be back soon. I quietly made my departure as soon as politeness permitted and left for home with my driver. I found her patiently sitting near the gate. I opened the main door, hung the lock and key behind the door on the latch handle and we walked in. As a household practice, after unlocking we keep the lock along with the keys hanging behind the door on the latch handle. Nami's arrival acted as a balm to my hectic daily schedule as she can ease my household workload substantially, allowing me to relax a bit. Nami, the driver and I retired to our respective rooms.

While changing, I thought of keeping the mangalsutra back in the almirah and wearing my regular gold chain. To my utter shock and dismay, I couldn't find the gold chain in my bag. I emptied my bag over the bed but could not find it and was in panic. Distressed, I called out Nami and the driver. Together with the driver I checked the car, the footmats, the backseat pockets, but to no avail. My heart sank at the thought of losing gold, and I feared a bad omen. I tried hard to recollect the sequence of the events of the day, yet couldn't figure out where I could have misplaced the gold chain. I rang up Suprava Madam who was the President of Inner Wheel, which was the ladies unit of the Rotary Confluence. I requested her to make an announcement about my lost gold chain so that if anyone found it, they could hand it over to her. I also requested her to say that the gold chain belonged to her because I did not want to disturb my husband with this bad news and distract him from the club event.

The more I thought, the more unhappy I became due to my inability to find the gold chain. Tension led to superstition. I started cursing my fate and wondered why this had happened to me when I had not harmed anyone. The superstition that losing gold was a bad omen, made me extremely perturbed. In the human mind, failure to find a valuable article slowly casts a shadow of suspicion on the domestic help. Nami suspected the driver but I ignored her as the driver had been working with us for a considerable period and had always been very trustworthy.

Out of sheer concern for me, I could hear Nami muttering under her breath, 'How is Baba helping you when you keep chanting His name day in and day out? Why didn't He come to your help at this odd hour?' I didn't know what to say. Neither did I want to question the one on whom I had immense faith nor did I want to pacify the situation by giving her false answers. I was in a complete mental disarray when my husband came back home and announced the news of the gold chain of Suprava Ma'am being lost. I tried putting on a brave face but ultimately gave in to the tension inside me and confessed that the chain was mine and not hers. He was very surprised and disturbed on hearing the news. He immediately rang the hotel staff with whom he had become quite friendly owing to the weekly meetings and requested them to do a quick and thorough search. But the hotel staff found nothing.

Monday was a holiday, but the two days of holidays were affected by this event. My husband was working and clients thronged his chamber for their cases. Nami kept herself busy with household work and cooking. The part-time maid came to do the chores. The disappointment over the loss stayed with me the whole day. The next day I got ready for office and went downstairs to take the key that was still hanging behind the main-door since that fateful evening. The moment I touched the lock and key, I screamed at the top of my voice as if I had touched a snake. My shining gold chain was entwined and knotted on the lock like a serpent on a withered branch of a dried tree trunk. It had been there since the last two days. Many known and unknown people had walked through the doorway, yet the gold chain went unnoticed. The door was locked at night before we went to bed, yet it remained untouched and unmoved. The maid came and cleaned the whole staircase and the main door, still it was unnoticed by her. I called Nami and asked her to come down immediately. Upon seeing the chain wrapped along with the key, she was at loss of words and appeared as if she had seen a ghost. I asked her help to untie the chain. I remember it took a good 20–30 minutes to ease the chain out. It might look like a coincidence, but the style of knots told a different story, without a human touch to it – as if the intention behind the complex knots was to keep the chain safe from preying eyes so that it could return to whom it belonged.

The event served as the perfect answer to Nami's questions. From questioning His ability to ensure the welfare of His devotees, she turned into an ambassador of Baba. She narrated the tale over phone and spread it via word-of-mouth when she went to her native village. This led to several villagers becoming devotees of Baba. That incident not only made Nami believe in Baba but also gave her a first-hand experience of His benevolent nature and that He ensures welfare of his loved ones.

She did ask me about the chain being there accidently. I smiled and said, 'I know one Sadguru who only can make possible which looks impossible. He is our Malik. He is our very own, Shirdi Sai Baba.'

14

Round the Clock

Sometime towards the end of April 2010, the sun shone bright on my luck and belief when I was blessed with yet another chance to visit Shirdi. My belief was strengthened because of the smooth planning for the pious journey without any impediments. My good luck continued and my younger son Chintu readily agreed to come along. Apparently, the suggestion to Chintu to go for the trip came from none other than Smita, my friend, philosopher and guide in the world of Baba.

Before my journey to Shirdi started, I had been pondering over what I should be taking for Baba. The TV showed endless streams of devotees in the shrine paying their obeisance by giving valuables in the form of gold, diamonds, bundles of cash, etc., disrupting the mental balance of every middle-class person. Nevertheless, I held my sanity and decided not to get swayed by all this. I decided on offering a Tulsi malaa, i.e., a garland made up of holy basil leaves. With all my effort and love for Baba I managed to make quite a big garland, bigger than my expectations but smaller than Baba's grandeur. I wrapped the garland in paper and then kept it in a separate bag. I periodically sprinkled water to keep it fresh and scented for the one it was meant for. We left Bhubaneswar by train, got down at Nashik and then took a taxi for the last lap of the journey, reaching Shirdi early morning. We checked into our hotel, refreshed ourselves and went for the darshan.

All along the journey, my husband had been apprehensive about the fate of the garland that I had prepared painstakingly, over hours of sheer dedication. He was concerned whether I'd be able to offer it at the shrine after carrying it all the way from Odisha. He suggested that I should be in the front so that the prominent garland is noticed by the priests. Though I didn't disagree, I stuck to my belief that Baba was omniscient and He would do something or the other to take the garland.

I was near the Samadhi area when I realized that Chintu and my husband had been separated from me in the melee there. I was all alone and with much difficulty in the pressing crowd I lifted my bag and tried to show the Tulsi malaa to the priest. What followed next not only reassured and strengthened my faith in Baba but also open the floodgates of my heightened emotions. The priest smiled and asked me to pass the bag to him. I happily did so. The priest then sat down calmly to clear the chaadar or the cover which was already strewn with petals of love and devotion from the sea of devotees who throng the shrine every day to have a glimpse of His Holiness. I was happy to see that the length of my Tulsi malaa was almost the same as the width of the Samadhi. With utmost care, the priest placed the garland on the Samadhi. I was only a silent spectator. My streaming tears bear testimony to the gratitude that arose in me when Baba accepted the garland with the same love and affection with which I had made it and carried it all the way. Tears gave way to happy smiles when I finally bowed in obeisance and exited Samadhi Mandir, with nothing but a bagful of happiness and a heart filled to the hilt with satisfaction.

Then I remembered my husband and Chintu, whom I hadn't met by then. I tried to look for them at the exit gates and around, but to no avail. I didn't stray far, lest they were looking for me as well and panicked upon not finding me. It was early in the morning and having been caught between the pleasure of the preceding events and worry for my missing family, I thought I should solve the problem systematically. I sat down in front of Dwarkamayi, and told the vendor, a small boy, 'Ek cup chai dena.'

The little boy was handing me the cup when I saw a trembling hand, skin wrinkled with age yet its glow refusing to fade away due to the blessings of Shirdi, asking for the tea. She was an old lady. Without a second thought, I gave her my cup. She smiled, showing her missing teeth and blessed me by placing her hand on my head before leaving.

Then the solution to finding my missing family dawned upon me. I walked to the shoe-stand and found them there. Chintu decided to go back to the hotel. My husband and I strolled around the Shirdi temple, visiting all the holy places there. At around midday we proceeded to the Prasadalaya to have the much talked-about Prasad Sevan which caters to around one lakh devotees per day. I went ahead to join the less-crowded ladies' queue to get the meal coupons and asked my husband to stand near the waiting area lest the morning lost-and-found story was repeated.

Before I could proceed, my eyes fell upon an old man standing next to my husband, dressed in tattered clothes and rags who politely asked me for a meal coupon. I readily agreed to give him one and joined the queue. Upon returning, I handed a coupon to the old man. We joined the queue to enter the Prasadalaya, patiently waiting for our turn.

In the afternoon, we went to the Khandoba Mandir to pay our obeisance to Lord Khandoba. While walking back to our hotel, we came across a vendor selling chilled

Shikanji or lemonade. We asked him for two glasses of Shikanji. The vendor was about to hand over the glasses to my husband when we saw an aged person, wearing an orange kafni like Baba, with swollen feet, who begged for a glass. My husband gently gave it to him. He guzzled down the entire glass at one go and his eyes showed the glint of his thirst being quenched. He smiled and walked away silently into the swarming crowd.

We visited several small temples which have come up over time in and around Shirdi, until late evening. Before calling it a day, I suggested to my husband that because we were in Baba's place, we should have the last meal of the day at the Prasadalaya. My husband is a man of few words and he just smiled in answer. When we were about to proceed to the hall just after getting our meal coupons, an old man with dishevelled hair and sunk eyes and with threadbare clothes approached us for a coupon. We paid him ten rupees and requested him to get one for himself from the coupon counter as the serpentine queue was increasing every minute.

With full stomachs, content hearts and a day filled with the holiness of Baba, we made our way back to the hotel. All this while Chintu had been happily ensconced in the hotel room, with room service at his beck-and-call and the TV remote to use freely. He had relaxed the entire day, finding adequate time for enjoying, with nothing on his to-do list.

We freshened up and I started recapitulating and narrating the entire day, bit-by-bit, to my husband, happy with the thought that my Baba was with me throughout the day. I mentioned an excerpt from Sai Satcharita, which says that Baba would take as much Dakshina as He wanted. Baba shared in every action of ours that day, instilling in me a sense of belongingness towards Him. Every stranger who had approached us for a meal or a drink was nothing but

Round the Clock

a human representation of Baba. Before I came to Shirdi, I wondered about what could I, as a common person, offer Baba. Now my visit was about to end, with His constant presence throughout with me in my thoughts and actions. Soon the exhaustion of the day took over my husband and he dozed off to sleep after being a pillar of support during my day's adventures.

I was still excited and wide-awake, re-living the entire day in my head when I decided to dial 107 for room service. Thanks to Chintu's frequent calls during the day, our room number had become familiar to them. The person answering my call asked, 'Haan sir, aur kya chahiye?' presuming it was Chintu again. I just said, 'Ek cup chai dena' and then smiled, remembering I had said the same words at the beginning of the day at Dwarkamayi, where His divine play had begun. Indeed, all is well, if chai is well.

15

Only the Believer Knows Where the Ant Bites

My posting as the Branch Manager at Balakati Branch was a challenging assignment and a deeply satisfying experience. From a professional viewpoint, I had to be steady and steer my branch using the rudder of my previous experiences through the waves of customer dissatisfaction and vicious whirlpools of bad debts. I reckon I did a fair job since my bosses started calling my work as exemplary during branch review meetings. At the same time, at a personal level, I was in a state of bliss because calling on Baba on the way to office and back had become an integral part of my daily routine.

Amidst all this, the most trying thing was the to-and-fro journey along the unsafe Tankapani Road. Though Baba's temple provided me relief, the road was a lonely, deserted one, with many potholes. And the road which ran along the bank of the canal leading to my branch was an unpaved, dirt road. In spite of being warned by good Samaritans and locals many times, I continued using the road. I carried the belief in Baba with me and draped myself in the fabric of His holiness and devotion. My strong faith in Him made me believe that He would not let evil cast its eye on me since He was there to protect me all the time. From the viewpoint of a believer this abstract yet constant presence is the bright side of the phenomenon named Baba which is seen, felt, perceived and accepted over the course of time.

It was a typical July evening. The atmosphere outside was enveloped in the greyness of the rumbling clouds and the occasional strikes of lightning. While the young children were busy making paper boats for the expected rain, the adults had been crowding the shops to discuss their affairs over a cup of tea. The dimming light told me to wind up my work and leave for home without any delay as the stretch of the dirt road till the temple didn't have a single lamp-post.

Due to myopia, I have to wear spectacles all the time. I put on my helmet, cleaned my glasses and started the ignition, to head home. Though cautioned earlier, I still took the road which I shouldn't have taken. The dirt road leading up to the temple is a narrow, elevated stretch, with a canal on one side and undeveloped tracts of land on the other. The drive became a harrowing experience when the skies opened up with all their might. The rain reduced not only the temperature but also the quality of the road. The road which had become firm and hard by the continual passing of light and heavy motor vehicles, turned into a dangerously eroding and mushy piece of land. The pouring rain blurred my vision and when it trickled down on my spectacles, my sight became hazier. Adding to my woes were the several huge, goods-laden trucks with their headlights on high-beam coming from the opposite side, which went past me at full throttle. Each time that happened I got frightened, but I didn't let fear take over because being courageous is not the absence of fear but having the strength to face the fear. I stopped, removed my spectacles and tucked them in my blouse. I started again, expecting to see a little clearer, but it didn't help. Then two fully-loaded trucks on high-beams passed by, instilling more fear in me. Meanwhile the dirt road had now become an all-round bumpy experience due to the erosion at the sides and the pot-holes becoming pits.

Then I relaxed my mind, becoming oblivious to the chaos of nature all around and tried to focus upon my destination and not the journey. I thought of catching a glimpse of the temple top ahead instead of looking at the mud stretch on which I was drenched from head to toe. The silhouette of the temple top against the white light soothed my soul like the assurance of a parent to his or her troubled ward. Before I could drift away in the bubble of hope, the waves of reality splashed me in the face to burst my bubble when I realized my spectacles were missing. The thought of alighting from my vehicle to search them on the road by which I had just come appeared even more dreadful than not being able to see clearly. I presumed they had dropped off during the earlier bumps. Tears streamed down my eyes and I could taste the salinity of my misery on my lips while the dark road seemed like an unending grim phase of life. That evening had every element of despair built into it and my fate stood a mute witness to that nerve wracking experience. When the tragedy struck, like everyone else, even I had a question for the Almighty – why me? I had been devoid of any materialistic wishes or riches or quantifiable acquisitions, so why was I a victim in this inevitable play of trying times being choreographed by none other than one of His associates, Mother Nature!

A sea of questions crowded my mind. Why me, God? Will I be able to reach home safely? Will this road ever end? Why haven't I ever thought of making a second pair of specs? Why me, God? How will I work tomorrow at office? Just like one part of the revolving earth is sleeping in darkness while the other side is awakening itself to sunlight, likewise nights are prelude to mornings. We might fail to make the cut tonight, but tomorrow morning the sun shall rise and shine and so shall we. As mere mortals, our vision is fixed at our sight and not diversified beyond the seen.

Amidst the splattering rain drops outside and the mental unrest inside, I felt a stinging sensation around my toes. It felt like a tiny but persistent ant biting me. The deserted road didn't permit me to halt and check my toes. All this while, I had been driving my two-wheeler, though very slowly. I was near the temple now and the glowing temple top gave assurance and hope, replacing the fear which had engulfed me till then. I reached the temple and heaved a deep and long sigh of relief. The downpour hadn't stopped till then but my dark day did appear to vanish when I bent down on my scooter and touched something hard. I realized they were my spectacles. Surprised, I tried to look in the dim street light. My spectacles were near the left leg space, neatly folded. I was speechless with disbelief at what I saw. The possibility of spectacles slipping off the folds of my saree, and resting neatly folded in the inadequate leg-space, during the ride in the storm on a muddy road with frequent bumps and jerks due to pit holes was very slim. Very, very slim, indeed! Tears flowed from my eyes when I remembered how I had questioned Him and His powers to keep me safe.

I put on my spectacles and looked up to see the temple top glowing in the white light, between the towering, lush-green trees. All I could see and perceive at that moment was that He was shining against the backdrop of the dark, questioning minds of mortals. This experience diversified and broadened my vision to look beyond the unseen, feel beyond the unfelt and hear beyond the unheard, because every end is surely a new beginning. A change in vision is all it takes to see Him standing beyond the horizon of our never-ending expectations and near-sightedness of unquenched fulfilment.

16
Ma'am You're Next

The first day at any place, be it school or workplace, is both nerve-wracking and exciting, and 27 July 2009 was no different for me, when I stepped into the coveted shoes of a Branch Head at Balakati Branch. The welcome by the staff, though overwhelming, couldn't hide the responsibility of delivering from the word go. Among the numerous tasks on my 'to-do' list, the first task was migrating the branch to core banking solution (CBS), which was extremely challenging and demanding. There is no room for error, so I had focussed all my energy to accomplish this responsibility successfully. For almost a fortnight I, along with the CBS team members, sat late in the office, until the final day of migration.

During this difficult time, I remember getting a call from an unknown number. The caller introduced himself as an officer of Central Rice Research Institute (CRRI) and wanted to meet me. I agreed immediately. In a short while two officers came to my branch. Politely, they said they had got my contact from the Agricultural Extension Officer (AEO). They were organizing a week-long programme at Puran, a nearby village. They needed a banking person to talk about banking to the participants. 'Never say no' is my motto, so I agreed to give a talk. Over a cup of tea, my topic was decided as 'Agricultural Credit'. I took that opportunity thinking that this would provide a platform to create a visibility of my bank in the area. It was 10 December and my lecture was scheduled for 17, so I had seven days to prepare.

The more the 17 December date came nearer, the more nervous I became. Though I had participated in debate competitions in my school days, that was long ago. I could not get time to prepare for the topic because of my hectic routine. Out of anxiety, I rang up Mr. Mondal, the coordinator of the programme, to postpone my talk to another date. But he made me relax saying that my speech would be in the local language, Odia, as the audience was only the villagers. And I had to speak only for half an hour as there were other speakers for different topics. I gathered my courage and despite my busy schedule found time to collect some information and make brief notes about agricultural credit. The preparation was casual and not up to the mark as per my own assessment. Mentally, I got ready to deliver the lecture without looking for frivolous excuses to hide my unpreparedness. The only problem I felt was the speed at which I speak. It is so fast that my lecture would finish in 10 to 15 minutes with the material I had. So how I would manage the audience for 30 minutes? Would I get embarrassed before the audience as well as CRRI officials? Perhaps Baba listened to my prayers.

The day arrived and on my way to the bank I stopped at my usual spiritual stop, the Sai Temple at Tankapani road. I poured my feelings of nervousness and performance anxiety to Baba. I requested Him, 'Save me Baba from embarrassment before the audience.' That was enough for Him.

I reached office and waited for the CRRI team to pick me up for the event. The car arrived at my office on time.

When I reached the venue and stepped into the hall, I had a shock. The audience consisted of a group of boys who had been helping with the lunch preparations outside the hall, besides six or seven elderly villagers. The CRRI persons welcomed me warmly with a bouquet of flowers. The event coordinator accompanied me till the dais. A Senior Scientist was speaking on Water Management and Water Harvesting using PowerPoint slides, giving a lot figure and facts. I realized that the speaker was very competent and knowledgeable, but was not able to connect with the audience. Just then the coordinator leaned forward and whispered, 'Ma'am you're next!'

Amidst polite applause, the earlier speaker left and the coordinator introduced me. My feet and hands were cold. Hiding my nervousness with a smile I thought of Baba and started off by the customary 'Namaskar' in an Odia accent. I don't remember what exactly I had prepared, but I spoke on agriculture credit, bad loans and recovery. I also spoke about customers' needs and our bank's commitment to service. I was speaking with confidence and connecting with the audience as I used to do in my school days. The lecture type session changed to an interactive session. Periodically I heard clapping from the audience.

After a while I realized that the hall was full with audience. So much so that I could see people standing behind the last row since there was no place to sit. The same bunch of boys who were busy with lunch preparations outside the hall were now bringing chairs, carrying them over their heads. I have a funny memory of two lanky youngsters sharing one chair towards the left side of the hall.

Amidst all this, I forgot that I had exceeded my time limit without realizing it. The coordinator whispered that I needed to end my speech as the next speaker was waiting. Just then Mr. Mondal, the senior officer, came from behind and said, 'Ma'am you please continue. This is the first time people are listening and enjoying a session during our programme.'

After a while I decided to wind up, giving the assurance to the audience that UCO Bank was always with the agriculturists and villagers whenever they required any sort of banking help. Loud applause was resounding everywhere in the hall. I was surprised and so were the CRRI officials. I couldn't understand as to what caused such an awe-inspiring response, but I could compare the expressions on the faces of the organizers before and after my speech.

The day ended on a high note when the CRRI officials who dropped me back at the bank requested me to be their resource person till the time I was at Balakati Branch. I sat down in my chair and closed my eyes to think about the happenings of the day. I couldn't understand the huge response to my session. The feeling of being a direct recipient of such awesome appreciation is something that is tough to express in words. Then realization dawned on me when I remembered I had stopped at Baba's temple on the way to the event, and poured my heart out to Him. Whether it was my simple and easy speech or divine intervention that caused the large participation and my appreciation by the audience that eventful day, is up to you to decide. I can only remember one of His sayings: 'If you cast your burden on Me, I shall surely bear it.'

17

The Voice from the Other Side

As the frequency of my visits to the Sai Temple at Tankapani Road increased, I started discovering and getting immersed in the various rituals of Sai Baba. My involvement and participation in Baba's world became so deep that for me, a visit a day, kept my stresses away!

Palki Yatra is a common term for every Sai devotee as this is a weekly ritual performed at most Sai Baba temples. I was lucky enough to see it closely on one occasion and then it became a regular affair for me. My Thursdays were booked for Baba's Palki Yatra and giving it a miss was never an option. At times, I used to get so engrossed that I became oblivious to the timings, food, family and, most importantly, to the deserted road that I had to travel to reach home. Sometimes I got lucky and got the coveted chance of lifting the Palki. Having noticed my regularity, Happy, the young fellow who himself was a frequent visitor, suggested me to avail a Paduka Seva. Having no knowledge about this ritual, I asked Happy. He said that the 2011 calendar had come and I should request the trustees to allot a date for the Paduka Seva to me. He said that there was always a huge rush for the Paduka Seva, so bookings were made much in advance to avoid any confusion later. I wished both my sons could also be present that day. Happy suggested I should book

The Voice from the Other Side

the date first and if my sons were able to attend, it'd be nice or else my husband could do the Seva. But if I keep delaying, then I would not be able to get a date.

The next morning, after my pooja, I went to the temple office and requested the President to allot me a date for Paduka Seva. After going through his bookings, he allotted me 7 July 2011. Though difficult for me to keep a secret and not utter a word about what is stirring inside me, I did manage to keep my secret until June 2011. Then I discussed it with my husband. His immediate reaction was that it would be better if both Guddu and Chintu were home at that time so that the entire family could be a part of this Seva. But both my sons were supposed to come home for their vacations and stay up to 27 June only.

When the boys came, the house was full of laughter, food, music, fun and, most importantly, togetherness. Nevertheless, a wish growing inside me was to see my boys carrying the Palki on their shoulders and my husband carrying the lotus Paduka on his head. At times, wishes are so strong that one can even visualize them beforehand. These scenes were so strong that they appeared before my eyes frequently. Though the allotted date was in July, I requested both my sons to accompany me to the Sai Baba temple on 23 June, which happened to be a Thursday, so that they could at least carry the Palki on their shoulders. Even though partly, my wish would happen to some extent as 7 July was far away.

On the morning of 22 June, I was in the pooja room, hurriedly completing the pooja as I was running late for office, when the phone rang. Expecting it to be from some office colleague seeking leave, I answered the call. The caller said, 'Maa, Sairam! I'm calling from Tankapani Sai Mandir.' I was quiet as I didn't have any plan to offer any dress or anything else to Baba at that time. What the person said left me speechless. He asked if the Paduka Seva which was scheduled for 7 July for me could be shifted to 23 June as the devotee who was allotted that date had a death in his family and had requested a postponement. He asked me whether I could agree to the change. Tears were streaming down my eyes and I was completely speechless to the extent that I couldn't answer the caller properly. Somehow, I thanked him and said I was happy to agree. I was standing in the pooja room before Sai Baba's photo and I broke down in tears of happiness. I had no words to express my joy and indebtedness towards Baba. I completed the pooja, and rushed downstairs into the dining room to disclose the good news to my family. I screamed with joy like a child who had received his favourite toy. I told them about my wish that I wanted everyone to be a part of this Paduka Seva while doing the booking in November 2010 and Baba had blessed us. My husband had also wished the same when I had told him about the Seva. Just then I got a call from the devotee who had booked the Paduka Seva of 23 June. He thanked me profusely, expressing his gratitude and how much the Seva meant to him, now that he could do it on 7 July instead.

The day of Seva arrived quickly and the events of the day got firmly etched in our memories for ever. My husband carried the Paduka, and both my sons carrying the Palki on their shoulders, and I accompanied them. I was trying to mingle in the crowd, struggling to hide my tears and lose myself in the overwhelming satisfaction that seemed to overpower me at the moment.

My instinctive feeling that someone was listening to me and paying heed to my inner thoughts and wishes got confirmed yet again. Baba not only fulfilled my wish but also eased the way for the beneficiary who had booked for 23 June. Baba maintained the equilibrium by balancing out the wishes of two of his devout devotees. We wished, and He ensured that He commanded His emissaries to fulfil them. It was the voice from the other side that created a possibility out of an impossibility because that voice was of Baba and no one else.

18

Patience or Belief

While many people go out to enjoy themselves on a Friday evening in some restaurant or bar, I was searching for peace and serenity that evening in Baba's temple. I had been neck-deep in work because of the half-yearly closing during September 2010. Targets, statements and closing reports had been filling my head as well as my table. But luckily, I managed to complete everything within the deadlines.

After this hectic activity I decided to visit the Tankapani Sai Temple on that Friday on my way back home and sit for a while gazing at the calm and lustrous face of Baba to my heart's content. To avoid any unnecessary worry at home, I informed my husband about my plans and late arrival. Given the fact that it was a Friday, the usual rush was considerably less and the atmosphere around was serene with a few religious chants wafting through the air laced with the fresh fragrance of flowers. I went upstairs into the main hall where the life-sized idol of Baba is installed. I sat near the entrance door and read the sacred Sai Satcharita. Reading the Sai Satcharita was my favourite activity. Whenever I found time, I would read a few pages. It would give me a sense of satisfaction and calm my nerves.

The tranquillity was very soothing for any devotee. Baba was draped in a parrot-green dress and adding to the magnificence was a garland of white flowers. His sight was so captivating that it appears before me even now, while I'm writing this. I was concentrating on reading the Sai Satcharita and whenever I looked up I saw Baba. Each time the number of garlands on Him were more. Suddenly, I had a mad thought of testing Baba. I said to myself that if Baba can hear the inner voice of all his devotees, then He should also pay heed to mine. There were so many garlands adorning Him, I wished I could get one of them without having to ask the priest there. This would be a test of Baba. And with that wish, I started waiting. I continued reading, yet kept looking up to Baba with that wish inside me. It was around 8:30 p.m. but I still waited instead of being sensible enough to take His leave and go home, for the road would be deserted at this time.

My patience was at the verge of running out. Logic, the destroyer of all human desires, took over when I saw the time was almost 9 p.m. I decided to wind up and go home. I kept the Sai Satcharita aside, bowed with all my sincerity and paid my obeisance to Him. I picked up my handbag and was about to leave when something caught my attention.

It was nearing Baba's Seja Aarti time and the bearded priest was signalling me to wait a little and not go. He then asked me to come near the idol. With soaring expectations, I went quickly and tried to control the excitement which was raging inside. Would I get what I asked or was it something else? I reached near Baba and the priest took out the longest and loveliest garland around Baba and put it in a carrybag and gave it to me. He then asked me what I was doing there alone as it was already late and no one was around. I turned around and saw that there was no one in the hall and it was only I and my keenness to get a garland. The priest wished me well and hoped I would

Patience or Belief

reach home safely. I could only smile back, with tears in my eyes. I was speechless. I was sure it wasn't the priest but a manifestation of Baba who asked me caringly and with concern about my well-being, and blessed me to reach home safely. Baba had granted me my humble and simple wish of getting a garland. I was sure that He had observed my sincerity in visiting Him every single day without fail after travelling those deserted, unlit roads. For me it was like seeing the Almighty descend to earth to grant a common devotee's wish.

Was it Baba's miracle or a coincidence? Was it the conviction of my belief or the result of a patient wait? I leave it to you to conclude – either logic will take you through the maze of rationality or the strength of your devotion will steer you to Baba.

A Strike for Good

My fondness for Baba was increasing regularly. I had become full of devotional curiosity. I wanted more and more information on Him, be it from literature or TV shows. No matter where I was or what kind of work I was doing, the image of Him sitting with one leg crossed over the other, with that the innocent yet piercing look on His face, kept flashing before me. Whenever I read about a Sai Temple, I made it a point to visit it somehow or the other.

Once I came to know that the oldest Sai Mandir in Odisha was at Jatni in Khurda District, near Bhubaneswar. I remembered an old childhood friend Pushpanjali, who was also an ardent Sai devotee. Those days her husband was posted as the Collector of Khurda district. I called her and said I wanted to visit the temple. She agreed to come along, but we couldn't agree on a convenient date.

Within a week, the union called a sudden strike in the bank. Such strikes are not only a forced holiday but also come with a pay cut. With an unexpected holiday in hand, I started thinking of ways to productively utilize the time when, coincidentally, Pushpanjali called. She simply asked, 'Can we visit the Sai Mandir at Jatni today?' 'Of course,' I replied immediately. She asked me to get ready quickly as she would send a car to pick me up from my home. I hurriedly finished my household chores and went to the Sai temple near my house at Jay Durga Nagar. I had just finished my pooja when I met my friend Shanti. I told her about the plan. After initial hesitation, with a little persuasion, she agreed to come along. I came home and got ready quickly. The car arrived and the three of us started our journey to the holy Sai Mandir at Jatni. I was so excited about the visit that I had forgotten to have my breakfast and started the journey on an empty stomach.

Pushpanjali told us that she had sought the help from a college friend to locate the temple in the by-lanes of Jatni. Mr. Sajan Agarwal, the husband of Pushpanjali's friend, called and said he was waiting on the main road near the highway to lead us to the temple. We reached the spot where Mr. Agarwal had been patiently waiting for us. He said that though he was a resident of Jatni, and a trustee-member of a famous Tirupati temple as well, he had not visited any Sai temples in the area. So he had called up all the Sai temples to know about their operational timings so that our visit would be most productive. We reached the Agarwal home where we were given a warm welcome. We decided to move swiftly, as advised by Mr. Agarwal, lest the temples were closed after Madhayana Aarti.

We followed in our car, right behind Mr. Agarwal who led us through the by-lanes on his bike. My excitement was obvious. Finally, we reached the first and the oldest Sai temple in Odisha. For the first few minutes, I tried to absorb the serene and peaceful atmosphere of the temple. As it was around midday the crowd was sparse. An unsaid wish got fulfilled when the priest handed over the Aarti thali to us to pray and perform our rituals. We paid our obeisance to Baba and then quickly left for the second temple.

At the second temple, a Telugu lady was performing the pooja. She happily greeted us and offered the Anna Prasad. I swallowed the entire prasad at one go as I had eaten nothing since morning. I felt baba could feel my hunger and made sure I had something to eat at the earliest. We sat there for a while and noticed that the temple was only partially constructed. Mr. Agarwal was a respected businessman in that area, and immediately gauged the state of the construction. He assured the lady of providing support for completing the construction.

When we reached the third temple, Madhayana Aarti had just finished and the temple was being closed for Baba's siesta. We quickly bowed down and had a brief look around the temple.

We made a dash for the fourth and fifth temple. Though Baba reigned in my head, I was feeling famished. Every time I walk on the steps leading to any Sai temple, the excitement and happiness of seeing His calm gaze fills me with an undefinable and intangible freshness. Saturation is a far away when one is full of devotion.

After the temple visits, Mr. Agarwal invited us to his home for a quick meal. I had never been to a Marwari house earlier. Mr. Agarwal's was a large a joint family and all of them welcomed us graciously. They said that though they were staying in Jatni, they had never heard about Baba, but now our visit had made them aware about Him.

The lunch was delicious and every dish was made in pure ghee. I was very hungry and relished every item of food. Mr. Agarwal's aged mother personally served us one dish after another with a lot of love and affection. She kept refiling our plates constantly. The food was delicious and the hospitality was wonderful.

After that sumptuous lunch we talked a little about our visit and experiences. As we prepared to leave, they didn't let us go empty handed. They gifted us wall clocks and

A Strike for Good

incense sticks and said that had we not come, they would not have been aware about Baba's temples in their own city. Their hospitality left us indebted towards them for life. We bid them farewell with hearts full of contentment and gratitude and stomachs full of their love.

While returning, Pushpanjali and I talked of how things fell into place within a week of our discussion, without putting any extra effort to plan things out. The way the circumstances arose and everything worked out smoothly was evidence of divine intervention which can only be ignited by a pure wish which does not expect any returns. It is rightly said that pure desires are always fulfilled. When you pray without expecting returns, anything can become possible. Shanti, who was reluctant initially about the journey, saw a radical change in her life subsequently. She treasured every bit of the day with us and became ardent devotee of Baba. She now has Baba in her pooja room and is also an active trustee of the Sai temple at Jay Durga Nagar.

Today when I remember that day, I realize that neither the scorching sun nor the dusty by-lanes nor a hungry stomach could act as a deterrent factor when Baba was on my mind. A day with Baba was a day to cherish.

20
Booked for Life

There is a popular belief amongst Sai devotees that we can only visit Baba when we are called by Him. Luckily, I have been blessed to visit Shirdi more than twenty times till now. Despite so many visits, every time I leave the sanctum sanctorum at Shirdi, I have a feeling of being incomplete – a feeling that I've left something behind, something that is calling me again and again, something that needs my attention. Experiences have multiplied themselves in terms of nurturing my love and devotion for Baba and also increasing the vigour and enthusiasm to immerse myself more in His sublime world.

During the last quarter of 2011, my husband suggested that we should go to Shirdi in the new year. I had never gone to Shirdi during any festival period due to the heavy rush. It was obvious that during new year celebrations, devotees would swarm Shirdi, but I still booked our tickets on the eve of new year, i.e., 29 December, for a new experience under the umbrella of Baba. The ticket confirmation served as a signal that our wish to visit Shirdi during the new year would be fruitful.

Here I'd like to mention that despite visiting several times earlier, I had never booked a hotel in advance. It

Booked for Life

was always an instant choice after reaching there. We have stayed at several hotels near the temple including Dwarabati and Bhakta Niwas run by Shirdi Trust. Someone or the other used to arrange our stay. It became my belief that Baba would help in my stay. The agent who had booked my tickets in the Lokamanya Tilak train informed that he was also going on the same train to Shirdi along with his family. I wished him a happy journey.

My fondness and devotion for Baba can't be described in mere words. Each time I have a trip scheduled to Shirdi, I become extremely happy. I make it a point to share my happiness with each and every person who matters to me.

At that time, I was a faculty at UCO Bank Training Centre, so I had been assigned to take some classes every day. A day before the journey when I was busy preparing for my next class, my cellphone rang. It was my travel agent, so I didn't feel the need to answer it immediately. But the phone continued to ring, so I answered it finally. My agent asked me whether I had made any arrangements for my stay at Shirdi. I said no, since my usual practice was not to book. He said there would be a big rush due to the new year but I didn't pay much heed to him. Then he said he was unable to go as there was some medical emergency in his family and insisted that I should use the booking he had made for himself and his family. I hesitated to accept his offer. His booking was in Bhakta Niwas, the oldest building there built by Shirdi Trust, and the stay may not be comfortable. My husband preferred to stay at Dwarabati. My agent reiterated that the rush would be maddening during new year. All my well-wishers with whom I had spoken earlier had also said the same thing. So, half-heartedly, I accepted his offer.

On the day of departure, my excitement knew no bounds. I wound up work in the office early, lest I was late for the train. The travel agent called and said he had sent the hotel booking receipt through a runner. I thanked him and hung up. Still not convinced, I decided to keep the receipt out of sheer politeness but not to use it. The runner came and I put the envelope into my bag without having a look and left office immediately.

The energy level in our train compartment was high. The compartment was full of devotees going on the holy journey to Shirdi. The journey being a long one, small conversations turned into long discussions about everything under the sun, starting from politics to sports, food to family but most importantly, Baba and His experiences. The air was full of talks about Baba and His miracles. Everywhere in the compartment small clusters of devotees shared their personal tales while others listened to them patiently, with full attention. I remember a lady saying she had not experienced any miracles. Of course, all miraculous experiences are subjective in nature and not objective. Eventually, everyone discussed their place of stay and its distance from the temple. I shared my practice of not pre-booking anything but enjoying the experience of everything falling into place on its own.

I suddenly remembered the envelope given by the travel agent. I took it out from my bag and opened it. Surprise awaited me, because the booking wasn't for Bhakta Niwas but for a two-night stay at Dwarabati. I was so happy that I shouted loudly and literally shook my husband.

As the train rattled through the night, I remembered one of Baba's sayings – Look at me and I'll look at you. Yet again, He proved His presence to those who choose to look at Him. It is your vision as a devotee that makes you look at things around you from the lenses of devotion and not the eyes of a rationalist. That receipt was a booking for two nights at Dwarabati, but that incident booked me as Baba's devotee for life.

21

Omniscient

When I happened to ask one of the persons standing ahead of me as to what this queue was for, he said, 'Yeh line Baba ke Naibedya Prasad ke liye hai, aap bhi khadi ho jaiye.'

With the new year of 2013 around the corner, my husband and I decided to be in Shirdi on the eve of new year. We made the arrangements and started our pious journey on 28 December 2012. During new year, Shirdi is overflowing with devotees from far and wide. The rush is maddening, and the devotion reaches feverish levels. Only the one who's a part of the crowd would understand the swarm of teeming devotees. Baba had correctly said once that Shirdi would be a place where people would throng and fill the place like ants.

We reached Shirdi and immediately joined the queue for the Sandhya Aarti. The devotees had come in huge numbers from all over, with the hope of worshiping Baba up close, resulting in slow movement of the endless queues. Due to the slow movement we couldn't reach the Main Hall of the Samadhi Mandir. We were stuck in Hall-2. Thanks to the numerous LCDs mounted in the hall, we enjoyed the evening darshan and Aarti through these LCDs, along with other devotees. During the entire Sandhya Aarti, my eyes were fixed on Baba's Naibedya Prasad. I noticed that Naibedya Prasad was offered only to Baba and then kept on the side, covered in a golden plate. I had a wish to have that Naibedya Prasad. I started thinking of ways to do that, though it appeared impossible as thousands of devotees were present at that time. But I just didn't want to let it go. With this thought in my mind, I moved ahead with the queue and had my darshan of Baba.

During Seja Aarti or the night prayer before Baba goes to sleep, my husband suggested that in order to avoid the rush we should sit and pray from Lendibagh. I readily agreed and we sat on a bench there and prayed. After the Seja Aarti the security staff wanted us to leave as the temple was about to close. We walked to the Udi counter and saw a huge queue. It was around 11 p.m. I wondered what it was about. My husband advised to go back to the hotel as it was getting late. But I was curious and asked a devotee standing there what this queue was for. He said, 'Yeh line Baba ke Naibedya Prasad ke liye hai, aap bhi khadi ho jaiye'. (This line is for Baba's Naibedya Prasad. You also stand in the queue.) I was speechless upon hearing those words.

We joined the queue immediately. The prasad was Suji Halwa. It was so tasty that I relished every single grain of it. While returning I was smiling to myself and my husband asked me the reason. I told him that during the Sandhya Aarti my eyes were fixed on the Naibedya Prasad and since then I had been thinking of ways to have it, and it seemed like Baba had heard my wish.

Maybe it was a coincidence. Maybe I just got lucky. But I strongly feel that our devotion is the sole way by which we can inch gradually towards our Almighty. Someone who believes in Him will see everything through the prism of His omnipresence as anything and everything that passes through that prism is nothing but His blessings in countless forms.

22

Omnipresent

It was few days before 26 January 2012 when the thought of completing Sai Parayan came to my mind. It was a daunting task of completing it within a day but nevertheless I firmly decided to make most of the national holiday. Coincidentally, the holiday was on a Thursday and it was a perfect day to perform one-day Sai-Parayan. Earlier, it had been pleasant and satisfying, though challenging, to complete the holy book in one day.

One day earlier, I recollected the belief in devotees that our wish gets fulfilled immediately when we successfully complete Sai Parayan. In my mind I told Baba – I'm thankful for everything You've done for me and this time I want your darshan, just darshan and nothing else.

Fuelled by the wish of getting His darshan, I completed the Sai Parayan on that Thursday. During the entire time of Parayan and after that, each time the doorbell rang, I thought it was Baba in some form or the other. I couldn't stop my impatient mind which kept wandering and looking out to see Baba. The next day, on my way to office, I kept looking around frantically on the road to get a glimpse of Him. But I was disappointed. It was tough for me to accept this anti-climax, but I did thank Him for all that He had done for me over the years and tried to be satisfied with that. The day continued with the usual banking work and my thoughts for a darshan somehow took a back seat and eventually faded.

The following day my younger son Chintu was arriving from Kolkata after completing his internship, so we went to the railway station to receive him. As his train was late, I was walking up and down the platform to pass time. Suddenly, a red coloured, hard-bound book displayed by one of the vendors caught my attention. I halted and leaned to have a look at the book. It was a book on Sai Baba titled *From Shirdi to Kendrapada*. I immediately purchased the book and started reading it under the faint light at the platform.

Meanwhile Chintu's train came and I saw him alighting from his compartment. He had three bags, so each of us took one. As we walked down, I was a little behind my husband and Chintu. Then I saw a tall person clad in a saffron coloured Kafni (like Baba) and a cap on his head, standing near the information board and looking at the chart. We had an eye contact with each other for a moment and he gave me a pleasant smile. He looked completely like Baba. I thought of stepping forward and touching his feet but hesitated due to the strangeness of the situation. My devotion told me to go forward and touch his feet, but reason and logic stopped me. Then Chintu turned around and asked me to hurry up. I pulled the trolley bag and walked quickly to catch up with my husband and son. When I turned around and looked back, that person was still there, looking at me and smiling.

We reached home and I got busy in the kitchen but the person's smiling face and appearance continued to fill my head. The following morning at the breakfast table, I described the incident to my husband and Chintu and asked them whether they had seen him. They said a firm 'No'. The turmoil within me continued. I asked them again that

Omnipresent

when I could see him, how couldn't they? But both were absolutely clear. They hadn't seen anyone as I described.

For the next few hours, that person's smiling face and the question why my husband and Chintu had not seen him seen him kept coming to my mind. In that confused state I went with them to Chintu's law school in the evening. While returning, I had my Eureka moment and gave a loud scream of joy in the car. My husband was obviously surprised. I excitedly told him that the person I had seen at the station was none other than Baba! On the day of Sai Parayan, I had wished to have a physical darshan of Baba and Baba had come to me. I am not sure how much my husband believed me, but I was totally convinced that the smiling face was no one but Baba manifested in human form.

This belief was reconfirmed the next morning. I was at the Sai Temple reading the Sai Satcharita. It was my usual practice to read a few pages, selected randomly, for 10 to 15 minutes when I sit silently at the Sai Temple. That day the book opened at chapter 29 and all my doubts got cleared. In fact, those who believes in Him believe that 'He is formless and everywhere.'

I smiled in peace and contentment. My restlessness and confusion within were settled and this also rekindled and strengthened my faith in Him.

23

Eternalized Mortal

My friend and guiding light Smita, who showed me the path to the beautiful world of Baba, often told me about various rituals related to Baba like Maha Abhishek, Pran Pratistha, etc. After such conversations, a strong longing was created within me to be a part of all such rituals. Luckily, I was blessed to see the Maha Abhishek at Tankapani Road Sai Temple but Pran Pratistha was pending in my wish list for a long time. Finally, one day, the wish to witness Pran Pratistha done by Guruji Dr. Chandra Bhanu Satapathy came true.

One day, during my stint at Balakati Branch, Mr. Panda, a colleague, asked me whether I was aware about the Pran Pratistha at the Gudia Pokhari Sai Temple. He said that the roads heading to the temple were heavily decorated with flowers, impeccable lighting and banners announcing the august presence of Guruji Dr. Chandra Bhanu Satapathy who would grace the occasion. I immediately decided, without a second thought, to go there for the hallowed ritual which was to be performed the following day. When I enquired about the route, Mr. Panda said that the temple was 3 km from our branch and situated on the left side of the Bhubaneswar-Puri main road. I decided to announce my plans to my branch staff as the onus to handle the following day's affairs would be on them, in my absence.

Eternalized Mortal

The next morning, with big expectations, I drove to the temple in my small Nano, which I had purchased a little while earlier.

I reached the temple on time and witnessed Guruji performing the Havan. Given the thin crowd, I could easily move forward to have a closer view of the ongoing ritual. Such close interface with the much longed-for Pran Pratistha cast a spell on me. The serenity and silence around filled my soul. After the Havan the Pran Pratistha or the installation of Baba's idol was performed. This was followed by Maha Abhishek, Chakhyu Daan, Bastra Paridhan and Aarti. Being a silent yet contented witness to the revered holy rituals of Baba and the august presence of Guruji from such close distance, I was on cloud nine. I still have goosebumps when I remember the scenes and re-live them in my head.

The rituals finally came to an end. During Prasad Seva the strength of the crowd increased suddenly, causing a traffic jam. I took the Prasad and came across a few of my bank's customers. Then reality dawned on me and I decided to go back to my branch, though reluctantly, after having spent half a day, with my whole heart, with Baba. Well, work is worship but I suppose worship had become work for me then!

After a few days my niece called and asked if I had paid a visit to Gudia Pokhari Sai Temple for the Pran Pratistha. I said yes and asked her how she knew about it. She said that an article has been published in *Sai Nirmalaya* magazine along with several pictures and I featured in one of them. My smile widened, the already deep satisfaction in my heart deepened and I saw the smiling face of Baba in the portrait in my cabin. He had sent His emissary in the form of Mr. Panda to tell me about the Pran Pratistha so that I could attend it and eternalized a mortal like me in one of the monthly magazines, for times to come. I looked at the energetic yet silent eyes of Baba, which spoke volumes without even uttering a word. Jai Shri Sai!

24

Counting on Hope

At times when we get a chance to be a part of something that we have seen earlier as an image or in a movie, we try to grab the opportunity and live every moment like it's the only chance we've got.

Long ago, during the early stage of my progress in devotion towards Baba, I had seen a scene on TV. Bucketful of currency notes and coins were being poured on the ground while devotes counted and sorted them under high security. Somehow the sight not only left its imprint in my mind but also intrigued me.

Sometime around mid-July 2011, my husband and I were travelling to Shirdi by Konark express. We were crossing Berhampur when my husband started experiencing stomach problems which eventually turned into the dreaded diarrhoea. Getting loose motions while travelling is always terrible. My husband started feeling weak and suggested that I continue the journey alone while he would return home. The sudden turn of events made me feel helpless and worried. So, without waiting for a moment, I made my distress call – I started to pray to Baba. Luckily, a group of medical representatives were travelling in the same compartment and were very helpful. They called the TT

Counting on Hope

who arranged for a doctor at the next station. The doctor assured me that it was not serious and my husband would be well soon. He remarked, 'Don't worry, things will be fine because you're going to Shirdi. Baba will take care.' By the grace of Baba, we reached safely without any more complications.

Upon reaching we freshened up and had darshan on the first day itself. My husband then decided to go to the hotel to rest. Next day, early in the morning, I decided to roam in the temple precincts and have a darshan all by myself. At gate number 3, it was inscribed 'Mukhdarshan'. I went in and saw that from there I could see Baba from a distance without having to go near the Samadhi. Suddenly I had a deja vu moment. I saw a scene from my memory being enacted – buckets full of currency notes and coins were being poured before devotees who were busy sorting and counting them under strict supervision and high security. I came to know then that this was a kind of Seva rendered by devotees.

In that hall I sat next to an elderly couple with my Sai Satcharita. I had decided to read a few pages in the serenity of the cool morning. After a while I saw the elderly couple get up and go towards the security guard at the central hall where the counting of money going on. They spoke softly to the security guard and he let them in. Without trying to understand what happened, I just followed suit. I decided that this would be my shortcut to get a clearer and closer darshan of Baba. I walked up to the security guard and requested him to let me in. I clearly remember his reply, 'Would you like to render some service to Baba?' Instinctively, I said 'Yes,' without even waiting a second. He said that I must spend an hour in the central hall and take part in the note counting service and then I would be permitted to have a direct darshan of Baba, along with the other devotees present there.

For a banker sorting and counting the money is a routine activity and I was quite happy to do it. After completion, I had the revered opportunity of inscribing my signature against my name and number on the register as a token of acknowledgement. Then, along with other devotees, I had a direct darshan without having to stand in the queue. While walking towards the Samadhi, I mentally wished for a rose from Baba's Samadhi. Indirectly, I was subjecting Baba to a test. Maybe He could read His devotee's mind and grant the wish. As I went forward with others, I kept repeating the wish for a rose in my mind. The priest who was standing until then, sat down near the Samadhi and the person ahead of me requested him for a rose from Baba's lotus feet. In response, the priest then asked us to pull the rose garland all by ourselves. I couldn't understand what he had just said so the priest repeated it. The moment he repeated his words, I pulled the garland with all my effort from the Samadhi. My joy knew no bounds when I realized I had an entire garland of roses and not just one.

I literally ran back to the hotel to share my good fortune with my husband. Upon reaching, my happiness doubled when I realized that the garland I had got was actually two garlands intertwined in each other. Having got more than what I expected, I closed my eyes for a silent prayer and thanked Him for the roses as a token of Sharadha and Saburi, i.e., love and patience.

My second stint with note counting Seva came quickly after that. It was during my subsequent visit to Shirdi on 21 December 2012. I had thought of performing the Sai Satyabrat Pooja and Sai Abhishek but due to Christmas and New Year, everything was pre-booked and the devotees thronged the places in huge numbers. With gloom writ large on my face, I thought of returning from the Satyabrat Pooja hall when one of the organizers called out from behind and handed me a big brass plate containing several small idols of Shri Krishna and Shri Ganesh. He asked me to place one idol in each of the plates kept in that hall.

Counting on Hope

Immediately, I felt a surge of happiness run through me as I was given a chance to do some Seva and nothing is more valuable than being a part of the worship. I placed the idols as directed. I turned to inform him to have a look when he offered me some prasad. I felt happy, yet a small spot of discontentment was lurking somewhere.

On the day prior to our return, I went to the temple for another darshan. I felt sad that I couldn't perform the Sai Satyabrat Pooja and Sai Abhishek, so I thought if I got a chance for doing the note counting Seva, I shall have no discontentment. While my husband and I were entering through gate number 3 for Mukhdarshan, I noticed that the note counting from Baba's Hundi (Dan Peti) was about to start. I went forward to the central hall and was automatically summoned by one of the persons who was selecting people for this service. Luckily, my husband also got a chance to do this Seva.

I have been fortunate enough to get the coveted chance of being a part of this counting process four times until now. The last two were when I visited with Manju during December 2017 and with Gita and Nicky during September 2018.

I believe when you expect less, whatever comes your way feels more. So, all these times, I have been counting on hope, hope to be closer to Him, hope to do something for Him, hope to be a part of His journey, hope to get involved in His divine world of faith. I received His blessings all the time, blessings which whisper to me every single time to never stop believing and to never lose hope.

The hope of yesterday and the belief of today can get us His blessings for tomorrow.

25

Throwback Thursday

When habits become your daily lifestyle, it's tough to change them. One such habit that has stayed with me all this while is listening to 'Living with Sai' early morning after I wake up. 'Living with Sai' is the divine rendition of a single man's devotion, love and faith for Baba – he is none other than Dr. Chandra Bhanu Satapathy, who has donned many hats, including as a composer, lyricist and vocalist, amongst many others.

It was a one of those cold wintry Delhi mornings where you are comfortable inside your home but get chilled to the bone if you dare to go outside. I had woken up early and was quietly preparing tea when I heard the Bhajan 'Mujhse haath na chudieyo sadhguru, sadhguru kabhi alag na kariyo' coming from somewhere. I took my tea cup and sat on the couch while aimlessly going through my social media posts and quietly singing the Bhajan. Suddenly I realized that the following week had a couple of holidays clubbed with the weekend. I called my friend Manju and we made a plan to visit Shirdi. I made the train bookings for 25 January 2017 departure and 28 January return and room reservations at Sai Bhakta Niwas.

Manju and I also spoke of a visit to Bhimashankar which has the oldest Jyotirlingam, and Trimbakeshwar. This was just a fleeting exchange of thoughts during the phone call and nothing was planned because Bhimashankar is approximately 125 km away and the journey is through a tough mountain terrain. Shirdi and Bhimashankar are in opposite directions from Pune. Due to all such issues, we didn't think of including these places in our travel plans. But we did want to go there.

Two days before my departure, I requested my MD to sanction a two-day leave for my trip to Shirdi. He happily approved my leave and gave me a small amount to donate at Shirdi on his behalf. He asked me about my travel plans and who I was going with, since my husband stayed in Bhubaneswar. I told him about Manju. He was a little worried, and being a kind-hearted person, he called a lady AGM of the bank, posted at Pune, and requested her to help us. Soon I got a call from her and I shared my detailed travel itinerary. She booked us in the SBI guest house at Pune and arranged for a vehicle to receive us at the airport and take us to Bhimashankar. She said we should carry some lunch and snacks as the journey was long and difficult, through mountainous terrain and the roads were not in good shape. There were no hotels or restaurants on the way. I was happy that things were falling into place, which was all a result of divine intervention.

When we reached Pune airport, the driver was waiting for us. We left for Bhimashankar and had a splendid darshan, all thanks to the unseen hand of God and the lady AGM. We left Bhimashankar on time and reached the SBI guest house at Pune, had a quick dinner and headed straight to Shirdi by taking the 10 p.m. bus. Before leaving for Shirdi, we thanked the lady whole-heartedly for her help and support. She had a lot of goodwill in the Bhimashankar area and we told her about the good things we had heard about her.

Though the bus ride was tiring, the morning air of Shirdi seemed to ease the exhaustion from our bodies. We freshened up quickly and had a quick darshan at Dwarkamayi. Then we hailed a taxi and left for Trimbakeshwar. Along with Trimbakeshwar, we also paid a visit to Panchabati and Sri Ram Mandir at Nasik, which were on the way. Our strong desires kept our tired bodies motivated and we managed to return to Shirdi by the evening. All throughout the return journey, I thought of seeing the Palki Yatra upon reaching Shirdi as it was a Thursday. Though I had already seen it at Shirdi many a times earlier, but nothing can quench the thirst of seeing Him in His myriad forms, again and again.

Upon reaching Shirdi, we saw that the place was full of devotees. It was a Thursday and 26 January as well, so it was a national holiday due to Republic day. The crowd made the chance of a darshan of Palki Yatra low. Nevertheless, we went through gate number 3, which is generally closed during evening Aarti, to have a Mukhdarshan. Luckily the gate was open. In fact, a surprise was in store for us. When we were standing behind the railings of Dwarkamayi, we saw that the Palki was right in front of us. The sight was a treat to our eyes and hearts. The Palki was being decorated by the sevadars inside Dwarkamayi. From placing of the Baba's photo to keeping the Paduka in the Palki, Manju and I saw everything from a very close distance. I was exulting from within but had composed myself to relish the experience.

All good things come to an end and our day ended on a high when we saw the Seja Aarti and had Baba's prasad. We went back to our rooms happy and at peace.

Early next morning we proceeded to Lendibagh. There I made a Rangoli using organic colours and placed our diyas on it. We followed it with our visit to Gurusthan, Parayan Hall, Ganesh, Shani and Shiva temples, which are

Throwback Thursday

all within the premises of Shirdi temple. Finally, we went for Mukhdarshan again and got the opportunity of rendering our services for the note counting process. While counting the money from the donation box, we had an uninterrupted and direct view of Baba. Before leaving for our hotel Sai Bhakta Niwas to re-live the events of the day we had a satisfying and sumptuous prasad at the Prasadalaya.

The next day we had to leave early to catch our evening flight from Pune, but my heart didn't want me to go without having one last look at Baba. We proceeded to have a last darshan of our trip via the biometric pass system and from there directly headed to Pune airport to catch our flight to Delhi.

Back in Delhi, the next morning I was back into the routine of daily life. I played 'Living with Sai' on the music system, poured tea into a cup and sat down on the couch to reminiscence the events of the last few days at Shirdi. I realized my unplanned trip turned out smoother and fuller than ever before. We visited every place we could have thought of, and the visits in and around the Shirdi were soul-satisfying. I felt as if an invisible, guiding presence paved the path ahead and readied the next step for me throughout the trip.

I smiled to myself when I realized that the lyrics of the song playing coincided happily with my thought. The lyrics 'Mujhse haath na chudieyo sadhguru, sadhguru, mujko alag na kariyo' were perfect and described the magical moment – 'My perfect master never leave my hand and never leave me alone'.

26
Essence Matters and Not Appearance

Right from childhood, I liked gardening. I used to enjoy picking flowers for my mother's pooja. Gradually I learnt the art of making garlands using flowers of different shapes, sizes and colours. In the course of making these garlands, I learnt something invaluable, something that has stayed with me till today. I learnt that a sense of cohesiveness can win over a sea of differences. Just like the string which holds all the different flowers together, our approach towards animals, humans and Baba can bring us closer to them and connect with them at a personal level.

The construction of our house at Bhubaneswar commenced in 1991 and a year later we shifted there. During the period of construction, I had planted several kinds of flowers, fruits and vegetables. After we moved in, the whole area was a treat to the eyes as the plants had grown well. One of the vines I had planted was the Aparajita flower, also called the Asian pigeonwings or bluebell vine. These flowers are blue in colour and are usually offered to Lord Shiva and Shani Dev on Monday and Saturday respectively. The plant had grown massively and had painted its surroundings in a sea of blue. The vines had almost grown to our balcony, which gave a beautiful and aesthetic appeal to the building. Often passers-by would stare in astonishment and then request some flowers. I

Essence Matters and Not Appearance

made a garland of these flowers and regularly offered it at the nearby Shiva temple. The priests were usually amazed at the size of the garland. With time, the plant aged and merged itself with Mother Earth, its creator. So I had been on the lookout for the same species of flowers for some time, but without success.

During late 1980s and early 1990s, I had not interfaced with Baba. One day when I looked at Him, I tried picturing the blue Aparajita garland against His snow-white idol. I had a wish to offer Him a garland like that. On my way to the Balakati branch, I would pass by the Sai Mandir on Tankapani Road. I had often noticed these blue flowers growing in the temple compound. So I decided to get a plant from there. On Saturday, while returning home from office, I stopped at the temple. There were a few gardeners busy trimming the shrubs and trees. They had thrown few saplings of Aparajita aside. I requested them to give me one of them, to which one of the gardeners replied, 'Why just one? You can take as many as you want, but mind you, these are from Baba's garden.' I instantly responded, 'What else can I do with these flowers except offer them as a garland to Baba?'

I took four saplings and planted them in my garden. While two failed to grow, the other two did very well. They not only bloomed into large plants full of flowers but also made good use of the bamboo support to climb up to my balcony. I collected these flowers and started making garlands and offering them at all the temples in the vicinity – Sai Mandir, Jay Durga Nagar, Durga Maa Mandir and so on. The blue garlands started to draw good reactions from the priests and devotees. They were astonished because the plant gave only a handful of flowers in their backyards, yet mine was yielding huge quantities. When they enquired from me, I could never give them a rational reason of such a large growth and only smiled, remembering my reply to the gardener when I got these saplings, 'What else can I do with these flowers except offer them as a garland to Baba?' I believe my reply to the gardener must have reached Baba's ears and the flowers were nothing but a manifestation of His vast blessings.

Later, in 2014, when I had a chance to move to Delhi, I always had several questions. Will I get a chance to visit a temple in Delhi? Will I be able to get flowers and make garlands for Baba? Baba ensured I could do all this easily.

In Delhi, I commuted to office either by metro or by bus. Metro involved changing trains, so I preferred a direct bus to office and back. One day, while returning from office via Dhaula Kuan, I saw a trail of champa flowers growing alongside the road. The whiteness of the flowers contrasted the backdrop of concrete walls and blue sky and created a magical effect. The growth was so lush that they had extended down the road for a considerable distance. I wondered whether the busy people in this metropolitan city found joy in the beauty of flowers. I started imagining a scene where I was walking into the temple and offering Baba a garland made of champa flowers. Before I could continue the thought, the bus came to a halt and the conductor asked me to alight as my stop had arrived.

With every passing day, the wish started to grow. Meanwhile, I had already located a Sai temple nearby at Najafgarh near my apartment and went there a couple of times on weekends. Being familiar with the route now, I decided to collect some flowers on a Saturday morning and offer them in a garland at the Najafgarh temple.

My husband was in Delhi at that time. When I shared my plan with him, he encouraged me to go ahead. But then few questions came to my mind – How will I go alone to Dhaula Kuan to collect these champa flowers? What will the passers-by think about me? Will they think that I'm a lunatic? Just then the doorbell rang and my maid came in to do the daily chores. I told her about my plan and asked her to accompany me to Dhaula Kuan. She agreed. We reached the place and quickly collected the champa flowers. For a moment I had feeling of playing KBC's

Essence Matters and Not Appearance

'Fastest Finger First'. Nonetheless, we completed our task and hailed an auto back home.

I sat down to complete the other part of the task. With a Sai Bhajan playing in the background, I started to make a garland large enough to satisfy my wish. Then, after a brief siesta, my husband and I headed towards the Sai temple at Najafgarh. In the main hall of the temple, we joined the small queue. People stared at me in disbelief. For the first time, the stares didn't make the woman in me uncomfortable, but rather, I was swelling with pride. Here was I, a working woman, fulfilling my wish for Baba with all the effort and courage I could muster. I did not just purchase a marigold or sunflower garland from the temple shop, but made one by my hands after collecting the flowers. This was my originality, uniqueness and sincerity at its peak.

I walked up to the priest and handed him the garland. He happily accepted it and placed it around Baba while doing the necessary rituals. Baba looked awesome with a circle of whiteness donning him. The priest offered me prasad and asked me to carry some more in my aanchal. With gratitude I accepted it and decided to stay in the hall for a while. Suddenly, an old lady, maybe more than 80 years old, came up to me and profusely thanked me for the garland. She blessed me and said the garland beautified Baba greatly. I guess Baba like the aesthetic appeal of the garland as well as the sincerity and effort that had gone into it, so He sent one of His emissaries to convey to me what He felt.

Be it the blue or white flowers, my love for Baba has been the big constant over the years while everything else is transitional. Holding on to the intrinsic value of anything is much more important than its aesthetic appeal because essence matters and not appearance.

27
Never Wished but Always Granted

Baba is not only omnipresent in the lives of His multitudes of devotees but also omniscient about their well-being. Steered by sheer faith and guided by the urgency of the situation, He has made Himself available in myriad forms before His devotees to resolve their problems. This is referred in almost every reported experience of a devotee, whether written or verbal. His benevolence is recorded in the minds of His devotees and nests in their hearts. People pray either out of fear or for a favour and sometimes I'm no different. But usually my devotion and desire to do something for Him has never been in exchange for fulfilment of a wish but rather out of sheer love and happiness that is generated when I do something for Him.

During my stay at Bhubaneswar, I never found the opportunity to organize a Sai Bhajan at my home. Deep down somewhere it was an unfulfilled wish. After shifting to Delhi I saw that my neighbour, who was in the flat opposite ours, used to organize Bhajan Kirtan occasionally. Out of courtesy, she had invited me to join their spiritual group. Owing to office work, I couldn't do so. But one Sunday I had nothing much to do so I decided to join them. I prepared some Odisha-style sweets and took them with me. The Bhajan Kirtan was in the name of Lord Hanumanji. The group completed their rituals and then had the sweets I had brought as prasad. Before they left, I proposed to them to have a similar Bhajan Kirtan for Sai Baba. They agreed and said that I should arrange a similar type of prasad for them. I happily agreed.

After much deliberation I had chosen 22 April 2018, a Sunday, to perform the Sai Bhajan since during the weekend it would be easier for me to make the arrangements according to my liking. Besides, my younger son was going to Mumbai to celebrate his birthday with his elder brother, so I would have the house to myself. My neighbour agreed to take up the responsibility of informing all the members of the ladies' group. After office on Friday, I went to the local market to buy the requirements for the pooja. Just when I got an auto to go to my apartment, a big thunderstorm started. Meanwhile, Gita, a family friend, tried reaching me on my phone twice to enquire about my whereabouts. I was trying to take care of the numerous packets and with the noise of the auto, I didn't hear the phone ring. I reached home safely, though partially drenched.

Before entering my house I rang the bell of my neighbour to remind her about the programme. On seeing me wet and carrying so many bags, she was a little surprised. She politely enquired the reason of doing the Sai Bhajan and whether I had any particular wish to be fulfilled. When I said that I didn't have any such wish, she was baffled. Though she didn't say it, the question writ large on her face was, 'Then why trouble yourself in the thunderstorm to get all these items?' Well, like they say, some things are better left unspoken. Nonetheless, she assured me that all the members of the ladies' group would be there.

While I was unlocking the main door of my flat my phone rang. It was a call from Gita. I also saw there were some missed calls from her. Gita enquired if I was fine. I told her that I had reached home safely and would visit her once the rain slowed down.

By the time I stepped out to meet Gita, it was nearing ten in the night. Though she stayed right across the road, but venturing out alone at this late hour is not a sensible or safe option. Anyway, I reached her house and shared my plans for the weekend and invited her to the Sai Bhajan. She said she would come and also prepare some dish for prasad. While returning home, I felt happy, wondering where I found the courage and strength to do all this alone at such odd hours. Each time I find something challenging before me, all I need to do is take the first step. The rest is facilitated by an invisible presence holding my hand. It is a feeling that comes from my faith and can be felt by anyone who has surrendered before Baba completely.

Sunday arrived quickly and I started the preparations very early. I cleaned the main hall and rearranged the furniture, making enough space to accommodate the entire Bhajan mandali. I lit the Akhand Jyoti before the idol of Sai which I had placed on the centre table and put on a Sai Bhajan. Since all the necessary arrangements were completed much before time, I sat down in a corner of the hall and closed my eyes. I could feel His commanding presence everywhere. It was as if I was being teleported to every corner of my house along with the effervescence of the incense sticks and the soothing lyrics of the Bhajan that was being played. I was in a state of trance and wanted to continue staying in it. I just wished to enjoy the serenity as long as it lasted.

Gita and her daughter Nicky arrived early, along with the prasad. They rechecked if everything was in place. The ladies' group arrived on time and our rituals started promptly. Hymns were chanted and recited with all fervour and sincerity, followed by Sai Bhajan. The programme went on for an hour. This was followed by Prasad Sevan.

Never Wished but Always Granted

Before leaving everyone donated a small sum of money as an offering to Baba and said that it was their first time and they hadn't attended a Sai Bhajan ever before. Just when I was thinking of which Sai temple to donate the entire amount collected as donation, Nicky suggested that we should visit the Sai Baba Mandir at August Kranti Road. Effortlessly, a wish materialized before I expressed it. Strange, yet true! By the time we returned from the temple, it was quite late but sleep still eluded me because the events of the day kept repeating in my head for quite some time.

The next day was 23 April, which is Chintu's birthday. I wished him early in the morning and left for office. All through the metro ride and the whole day at office, I kept remembering the previous day's events. They just refused to go away.

When I was sharing my experience with one of my colleagues who hails from Chennai and sits next to my desk, a visitor called on him for some official work. The visitor greeted him and gave me a smile too. I smiled back and was trying hard to recollect if I had seen this person earlier. Before I could remember who he was, he said, 'Madam Sai Ram,' and handed me a ladoo prasad, an Udi packet and a picture of Baba, saying, 'This is for you Ma'am.' For a moment, I couldn't comprehend what was happening. Getting these things from a stranger, which were all a physical manifestation of Baba's blessings on the day following Sai Bhajan, was simply unexpected and surprising. When I stood up to distribute the ladoo prasad amongst my other colleagues, the visitor said that he had got prasad for everyone and that particular packet was specifically for me. Pleased with his sweet gesture, I got back to my desk and smiled happily to myself. Then I remembered that the person was a resident of Pune and had paid a visit to our office a year ago. He had then invited my colleague from Chennai to pay a visit to Shirdi. My colleague had told him that I was an ardent Sai devotee and went to Shirdi quite often. To me it seemed that since the preceding day I was continuously being showered by blessings, with every moment bringing a new set of joy and happiness bundled together.

After work I took a bus home. After I alighted from the bus, I had to walk a bit since the bus stop was at a little distance from my home. The road was lighted in patches but was predominantly dark. I was carefully walking by the side of the road instead of taking the uneven footpath. Suddenly, I felt a hand on my neck for a brief second and a quick, jerking action. Before I could fathom what happened, I saw a bike whizz past me in a flash. I realized the person had snatched my gold chain and had fled from the spot. I shouted out of fear and panic, and a crowd of bystanders gathered around. I was somehow calm and didn't worry about the loss of the gold, though it was an inauspicious omen. I held myself together as I was unharmed and unhurt in this unfortunate event. Someone amongst the crowd must have called the police as I saw the police gypsy coming near. Quickly, they took the details for a FIR. Then a policeman escorted me to my apartment and I thanked him. I regretted not listening to the warnings earlier from friends and colleagues about not wearing gold as such chain snatching incidents were on the rise. Then the magnitude of the loss and the risk to my well-being started to dawn upon me. But instead of breaking down, I decided to use the incident as a learning experience.

When I was about to reach my flat, I decided to call on my neighbour. I knocked on her door and she welcomed mè inside. I narrated to her the chain snatching incident. She was obviously shocked. Then she asked the question she had asked me earlier – what was my wish I wanted fulfilled after arranging the Sai Bhajan? I repeated my earlier reply that I had no wish. I completed my answer then by saying, 'Each time I wish to do something for

Baba, it is only out of sheer love and devotion. There is no wish or motive behind any of my actions for Him. I find joy, satisfaction and happiness in being a part of the process where I am doing some activity for Baba. But still, every time He grants me something or the other in His myriad ways. His presence protects me from any injury. This snatching incident could have spiralled out of control if the chain had remained firm and not broken and opened up – it was a thick chain. I would have got pulled by the neck by the robbers. Baba's presence has been following me like a shadow everywhere I go and in everything I do.'

I smiled at her. I felt lighter, happier and back to my normal self, as if nothing had happened. After that evening, I believe that my neighbour also started to be attracted towards Baba.

My actions for serving Him have never been an obligation but simply in response to a calling from within. Being a part of any activity which relates to Him is a blessing for me and I need no other fruits of my labour and love. It is easy to appreciate the magnitude of His blessings if we can see the difference between what could have happened had He not been there and what actually happened.

28

A Known Mystery

The appreciation of divine intervention starts from the point where intelligence gives way, medical science fails, and human understanding stops. When all the doors of every possibility are closed, the impossible finds a way to take place. This light of impossibility which is beyond human comprehension is nothing but the invisible presence of the omnipotent Baba. The magical effect Udi has on people who are plagued with some illness is a common example. A doctor would advise against consuming such ash, but those who have done so as a last resort, have conquered their illness after a long, arduous battle. The Udi might be medically questioned but spiritually, it is the panacea for all illness. I will narrate few stories that I have personally come across.

The first tale comes from Hurasahi, a remote village in Kendrapada district of Odisha, where my paternal home is situated. My youngest brother resides there and looks after our family home and the agricultural land. Having had his roots deeply embedded in a rural setup, he is a man of few words. Once while I was visiting him, he talked of a miraculous experience.

A Known Mystery

My brother had distributed small pictures and calendars of Sai Baba, which I had brought from Shirdi. One of the recipients was the school headmaster. He was happy to receive the picture and had neatly placed it on his table. He didn't have any particular reason to place it there, but he just did what came naturally to him.

One day all the schools in the district were informed that an inspection visit by the officials of the Department of Mass Education would take place after two days. The headmaster had to make a presentation and justify the expenditure incurred in completing the construction of the school building and provision of basic amenities to the students. The headmaster was worried because despite his sincere efforts, the construction work was not complete. He had a sleepless night thinking about the worst possible outcome for something which was beyond his control. He had mentally prepared himself for a stricture and a notice being served on him.

The following morning he kept a track of the movements of the inspection team. As the turn for his school approached, he became very nervous and sweat trickled down his brow. With folded hands he sat before Baba, requesting Him to save him from that situation.

Just then he got a call which left him dazed. The inspection team had to return immediately for some urgent and unavoidable work. The inspection of his school would be done later. The headmaster was completely speechless for a while and could not believe his ears. Needless to add, he visited Shirdi soon after this incident.

Just adjacent to our home in the village, there lived a person who did odd labour jobs to make ends meet. It was a hand-to-mouth existence because there was just one earning member and four mouths to feed. He had two daughters out of which the eldest was diagnosed with polio. She wasn't educated, which made the situation worse.

For that person and his wife, there seemed no end to their hardships. Nevertheless, the youngest daughter got married in a nearby village and the parents sighed with relief.

As fate would have it, the youngest daughter came back home after a few days in a completely insane state of mind. The parents were afraid for her future and grieving in sorrow. But in spite of the difficult situation, they didn't stop trying. They took her to every medical practitioner possible who could possibly cure her, but to no avail. All attempts to ease their or their children's lives was thwarted by fate. Having run from pillar to post in search of a cure, their hope was wearing thin.

Each time I go back to my village, my discourses about my experiences of worshipping Baba always attract audience in large numbers. One day while I was sharing my experiences, the mother of this girl was sitting there. Unaware about her situation, I continued talking. The girl's mother was so moved that she went home and started worshipping Baba with all her heart. After a couple of weeks, I got an excited call from my brother who said that that the girl who had lost her mental balance was recovering and was getting better. He said that the whole family had now started believing the Fakir, that is, Baba, completely.

The point I wish to make is that belief is the key to any change. The believer shouldn't lose hope and the non-believer should never stay away from believing. What might look impossible, might just be changed to 'I'm Possible' by Baba.

There were several such episodes which connected to Baba. They instilled a deep sense of faith and devotion in the hearts of the villagers towards Baba. There was increased happiness and a sense of security in their lives. Gradually, they didn't feel helpless about their problems any more as they found a ray of hope in Baba. They believed He was there to support them in any situation.

A Known Mystery

Once, before leaving for Shirdi, I happened to inform the details of my trip with my youngest sister-in-law, who resides in the village. She went ahead and shared them with the villagers who came to our house or resided nearby. One of them requested my sister-in-law to ask me to get them some idols and photos of Baba from Shirdi. But she didn't say anything as she was hesitant to ask me for this favour.

At Shirdi, just before returning, I went into one of shops and purchased around 15-20 idols and pictures. When my husband enquired, I replied that that I would distribute them amongst the people in my village. He smiled in approval. On my next visit to my village, I distributed the idols and pictures. The villagers were very happy but my sister-in-law appeared perplexed. She asked me if anyone had requested me to get these idols. When I said no, she recounted the story and the reason she had not requested me. I just smiled back and said the thought of getting them must have been planted in my head by His divine intervention. I was only a humble messenger of His.

My friend Sanjukta, who works in RBI, had told me this tale in Kolkata. She had never shared this experience with anyone but seeing my love for Baba, she talked about it.

Long time ago, during the late 1990s, she had got a pendant of Baba which she kept in her pooja room and worshipped it. Over time, Baba's face had blurred due to constant smearing of sandalwood paste daily during the pooja. So, one day she thought of cleaning it. Unfortunately, while washing it slipped from her hands and fell into the washbasin and then went down the drain pipe. Before she could react, it had already gone into the drain. Sadly, she didn't have any other picture of Baba. The incident not only left her worried and disturbed but also made her impatient as she kept having flashes of Baba's face before her eyes.

What happened next can only instil faith in the minds of a devotee and believer. Within a week from the fateful day she received an envelope containing a picture of Baba. The sender's address was blank, but the postage mark affixed said Bhubaneswar. She felt as if someone had heard her prayers and felt her sorrow. She put the envelope to her forehead and thanked the sender in her heart because she knew the answer to her query, 'Who has sent it?' would always remain unanswered. So remember, no matter how dark the tunnel looks, there is always light at the end of it.

One of Baba's sayings which has stood the test of time and is strongly believed by the devotees is, 'I shall be ever active and vigorous even after leaving this earthly body.' For Him, there is no end, but always a new beginning.

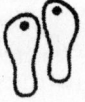

29

Down but Not Out

From an unknown to becoming an integral member of my family literally, Baba's place in my life has deepened over the years. His prominence and presence in my life has seen a huge rise. No matter where I go, I always try to find the nearest temple to where I am staying. My endless love for Him makes me look for Him everywhere I go. Luckily, everywhere I go, I find a like-minded person who is willing to help me and take me a step closer towards Baba.

In 2013, Koushik or Guddu, my elder son, got posted to Vizag on INS *Kalinga*. Vizag was near Bhubaneswar and with Guddu there, I had a good reason to take leave from work. The first time I went to Vizag, it was over a weekend for a two-day stay. Before going, I had asked Guddu to find a Sai Baba temple so that I could pay my obeisance before leaving the city. He happily agreed to take me to one. I had a pleasant stay but not having visited a Sai Baba temple created a feeling of missing something. While going to the railway station to catch my return train, I asked Guddu if he had found a temple for me. He said that he had tried but couldn't find one. Whenever he had driven anywhere in the last few weeks, he had kept a lookout on both sides of the road in case there was a Sai Baba temple. But he didn't find any.

I remember it was around 8.30 p.m. when I suddenly heard 108 Sai Naam being chanted somewhere nearby as Guddu drove me to the railway station. I exclaimed in excitement and asked Guddu to stop the car. He parked the car and both of us alighted to look for the source of the chants that soothed my soul. We found a huge idol of Baba nearby. We bowed down in obeisance and then left immediately for the station lest I miss my train. Guddu said that he had crossed that road and the junction where the idol was placed several times but had never seen the idol or heard the 108 Sai Naam.

After a few days Guddu rang up and informed that my next visit would be more enjoyable as he had found out a Sai Baba temple near his Naval Base at Bheemunipatnam, which also had an old-age home attached to it. He said that the peace and serenity of that temple would cast a spell on me.

Very soon, my husband and I visited Vizag to spend an extended weekend with Guddu. The first day itself he drove us to the temple. It was very near his base so a lot of naval officers frequented it. The atmosphere around that temple was different in comparison to other temples. There were no priests for the rituals or giving the prasad to the devotees. Having an old age-home attached to it, the temple was managed by the senior citizens who resided there. They were mostly retirees and had divided the work between themselves and performed everything very efficiently. Their old age might have slowed their pace but not their enthusiasm. They were happy to see us along with Guddu. All of them came from different places and spoke different languages like Telugu, Tamil, Kannada, etc. Words couldn't help our communication with them. But what words couldn't convey, their grieving eyes and sorrowful expressions did. Silence and action spoke on our behalf and their slow-moving hands gave more blessings than we could ask for. They were left at their own will by their families, yet they found a home under the umbrella of Baba. Separated from blood, united by Baba. They were happy with one another and found solace in the company of Baba.

Just before starting back, Guddu touched the feet of the inhabitants there and they hugged him out of love and affection. It was a moment of pride when a mother like me could see the result of all the years spent in inculcating values in him.

We had a pleasant stay at Vizag but upon returning I couldn't forget the faces of the old folks in the temple. The simplicity in their life bore a striking resemblance with the life of Baba, the Fakir.

Over the years, my bonds with the people of the old-age home deepened. Our silences and inability to communicate clearly brought us closer. Each time I went to Vizag, visiting the temple and the old-age home was a must for me. The people there became so familiar with me that at times they asked me to stay longer or give them a hand in preparing prasad. For me, they became an extended family. In 2014, when Guddu married Luis, my beloved daughter-in-law, I thought of gifting new clothes, sweets and toiletry kits at the old-age home as a token of love and respect. Luckily, this thought materialized in the best possible way when Guddu, Luis and I arranged the distribution of the gifts after their marriage.

I always kept a track of the old-age home in some way or the other. Subsequently, I found that their monthly rations were funded by an NGO and an ambulance was sponsored and donated by State Bank of India. I felt proud knowing that such generosity originated from someone in the banking fraternity. I met the kind-hearted officer who had managed this project. Though there was the same language barrier between us, but gratitude didn't require any mode of communication. Folded hands and teary eyes spoke volumes. I was so moved that during my last visit I bowed in gratitude and gratefulness before the name that was inscribed on a marble slab in the temple. It was the name of the founder who had constructed the old-age home, along with the temple. His vision is an embodiment of Baba's words 'Love, Kindness and Sympathy'.

The old folks were knitted together using the invisible thread of Baba's devotion and have truly found one another's company for their second innings. They belonged to one another under the watchful eyes of Baba. The problems of life may have tried to put them down, but they were definitely not out.

30

The Forbidden Fruit

Sometime in mid-2010, on a Saturday, I was at office neck-deep in work when I thought of paying a visit to Baba at Tankapani Road temple. As soon as I wound up work, I left for the temple. Upon reaching there I found an unusual rush for that time. As I walked in I heard devotees talking about Guruji. By then though I was very involved with Baba, somehow the phenomenon and persona of Guruji had eluded me inadvertently. Dr. Chandra Bhanu Satapathy, fondly addressed as Guruji, had come to the temple. He was considered as a living representation of Baba by the devotees. So, meeting him in person would be like meeting Baba and all the devotees were waiting patiently, with folded hands.

The queue was moving at a snail's space adding up to my exhaustion as I didn't have time to eat anything since breakfast and the scorching sun increased my discomfort. Then I saw a few devotees, who were not a part of the queue, being taken into the hall by the volunteers who were at the doors. Despite being irked at them, I thought of trying my luck and went forward. I requested the volunteer to let me in but he refused. With that I had no hope of meeting or seeing Guruji. Disheartened, I walked up the stairs, paid my obeisance to Baba. While returning home I consoled myself by thinking that even if I didn't get a chance to meet Guruji, I had Baba with me. But no matter how much I tried to console myself, not meeting Guruji was a slowly growing void within.

Later in the evening, when I was speaking with my friend Smita, she cut me short and asked me whether I had met Guruji. When I said no, she went on to talk about Guruji. Hearing her, the disappointment of not having met Guruji increased the void in my heart. Nevertheless, I didn't let it get the better of me and I put up a brave face.

In December 2010, I got a call from Mrs. Panda, Smita's mother and Trustee of Tankapani Road Sai Temple, to help in making arrangements for Sai Palki Yatra which would be performed by only women. She said that the Palki Yatra would be inaugurated by Guruji. That Thursday, I reached the temple and got busy with making the necessary arrangements for the Palki Yatra. A crowd of women devotees waited with folded hands to have a glimpse of Guruji. The accompanying men folk were around the temple and were also waiting for the arrival of Guruji. The moment he arrived, tall and lanky with a commanding presence, ripples of excitement ran through the crowd and shouts of 'Jai Shri Sai' went up in unison. Guruji then performed the requisite rituals to start the Palki Yatra.

The milling crowd encircled him. I could have a glimpse of Guruji only from a distance because of the heavy crowd. I consoled myself with that glimpse.

The women lifted the Palki and circled the compound of the temple as was the custom. Soon the programme came to an end, the offerings were distributed amongst the devotees and they started to disperse. I called out for my driver but was unable to find him. He had joined only two days earlier and did not have a mobile yet. Instead of waiting for him, I went back to the temple to have a

The Forbidden Fruit

look at Baba again. While walking up the stairs, I saw Guruji coming out of the Parayan Hall through the back door, flocked by an entourage of volunteers. I stood at the stairs to see him from near. For a moment I felt that Guruji also looked at me and said, 'I am coming, I know you are waiting for a long time.' Within no time Guruji, cordoned by the volunteers, reached the same stairs where I was standing with other devotees. The volunteers shouted to clear the path quickly and all the devotees left. I was dumbstruck and stood still, without moving an inch. No one objected to me and Guruji came to the stairs to go to the main hall. I bent down to touch his feet. He put his hand on my head and walked ahead. For a moment, time stood still for me because his touch was a direct blessing from Baba. What I missed a few days ago was more than made up on this holy Thursday.

The next time I met Guruji was at the airport sometime in October 2013. My husband and I were returning from Nepal and waiting at Delhi airport for a connecting flight to Bhubaneswar. There was an announcement for a gate-change of my flight. As I got up to walk towards the changed gate, I saw Guruji sitting at a distance and was busy writing something. A girl and a boy were sitting silently near him. I immediately ran towards him and touched his feet. He looked at me and asked politely, 'Do you know me? Where are you from?' I replied that I was from Bhubaneswar and there would be hardly anyone in Odisha who would not recognize Guruji. He smiled and said that he was busy in writing. Without disturbing him further, I took a seat near him with my heart fluttering in the excitement of being so close to him, in person. I sat silently with my gaze fixed on him.

He continued writing, but he did look up at times and caught my gaze. I felt as if he was reading my mind in those glances. The boarding announcement interrupted my silent and serene moments. Guruji got up and said to me,

'Let's go! We're co-passengers in the same flight.' I bowed down before him in gratitude.

I proceeded to board the flight with my husband but failed to locate Guruji after that. When I landed at Bhubaneswar airport, the trustees of Tankapani Sai Temple were waiting to welcome Guruji. Mr. Panda, Smita's father, asked me where I was coming from. Hearing that I was coming from Delhi, he said that I was really lucky and blessed to share the flight with Guruji. I just smiled at his words and didn't mention my meeting with Guruji at Delhi airport. The void of not meeting Guruji on that Saturday slowly started filling up.

When I shifted to Delhi in November 2014 after my transfer, I was anxious as how I would manage to visit Baba's temples in this huge metropolitan. I got the chance of visiting Shri Jagannath and Sai Baba Temple at Hauz Khas, along with my dear friend and extended family, Gita. She is a very holy and spiritual person whose company is very precious to me. By then she had not met Guruji nor visited Sai ka Aangan at Gurugram. So on 25 December 2014, just a few days after I joined the Central Registry under DFS at Delhi, we decided to visit the much talked-about Sai ka Aangan at Gurugram.

The incident that happened next was beyond our imagination. Upon reaching the temple we could hear a male voice singing Sai Bhajan inside the temple. Though the voice sounded familiar, we couldn't identify it. The moment we walked into the temple we were astounded to see that the singer was none other than Guruji himself. He was playing a harmonium and singing Sai Bhajans. Devotees had filled the place in huge numbers. Despite the crowd we managed to find ourselves a little place so that we could soak in that air of devotion. Once Guruji finished the Bhajan, he asked the audience which one he should sing next. I shouted from the back 'Iswar se kuch

The Forbidden Fruit

mangna hoto', a bhajan from Guruji's collection 'Living with Sai'. But my wish of hearing the bhajan live from Guruji could not be fulfilled as he was diverted with some other request.

After the evening Aarti, we went and touched Guruji's feet. He asked me if I had heard the Bhajan 'Iswar se kuch' on a CD. That meant he had heard my shouted request and recognized me even in the huge crowd! Happy with the thought, I replied that the bhajan was like my morning cup of tea as my day started with it every day.

When we left, Gita and I were full of happiness and joy. With Guruji, each time you meet him, you're left with a lingering feeling of completeness from within.

Being unable to meet Guruji on that Saturday afternoon became a wish I redeemed subsequently on several occasions. Someone has rightly said, what's yours will eventually find its way to you.

31

Faith Healing

My father served the defence forces, so my respect and fascination for uniform has always been big. I believe that influenced my elder son to serve in the Indian Navy and each time I see him in his much-respected White Uniform, I am filled with pride. Seeing him in uniform is a fulfilment of my father's desire, 'Pachi, why don't you send Guddu in fauj? It'd be nice.' During Guddu's posting at Vizag, I visited the place so frequently that it became second home. Every long weekend or national holiday was the best occasion for me, to be with Guddu. It was also the perfect reason for seeking an extra leave from office.

In April 2017, I was in Vizag to spend some time with Guddu. My husband joined us from Bhubaneswar. Chintu could not come for reasons best known to him or maybe he wanted to have some 'quality time' later with his brother and sister-in-law, without parents around. It was an eventful trip as Guddu took us around one of the naval ships that had docked there. It was an insightful experience from a civilian point of view, as we came to know about the working of a ship and the various functions of the officers, sailors and crew on board. It was not all smooth sailing as we see on television, because the efforts behind

Faith Healing

making a ship sail efficiently are enormous. We climbed several steep staircases to go around the ship. Sometime in between I felt a slight yet stinging pain in one of my legs. Thinking it to be something minor, I continued with the activity. The refreshing trip ended after a week and I returned to Delhi.

During my stay in Vizag, the pain in my leg was persistent but not unbearable so I didn't inform anyone lest they got worried. But during my stopover at Hyderabad airport I could feel the pain increasing slowly. I couldn't sit properly and kept fidgeting to find the position that might subdue the pain, but to no avail. In much discomfort, I reached Delhi and joined office the following day, limping a little. When I went to meet our MD upon his arrival, I couldn't conceal the agony written all over my face. Even he could sense something was amiss and asked me again if everything was fine. In the evening, after coming back home, the pain increased and became unbearable. I tried watching the television to take my mind off the pain but it was of no help. Somehow, I closed my eyes and tried hard to sleep. All this while I hadn't informed Chintu about my pain.

The next morning, I called up Dr. Ankita Das or Nicky, Gita's daughter, and narrated my problem. She said that I should immediately visit a doctor. Chintu took a day off from his office to accompany me to the hospital, along with Gita. Chintu is only tough from appearance but soft from within. He was very worried seeing the way I was walking in pain.

What followed at the hospital next is something that can only be appreciated by someone who has always been active. The hospital attendant asked me to sit in a wheelchair and took me to the doctor. I felt like a bird whose wings were clipped and then put in a cage. All of a sudden, dark clouds of mental captivity, physical incapacity and curtailed freedom loomed large. Before reaching the doctor, I was very fearful of the outcome. The doctor suggested diagnostic checks like X-Ray, CT Scan and MRI to know the cause behind the pain. The wheelchair session continued for some more time. When I requested the attendant to let me walk, he said their medical norms did not allow it. While I was being taken across the central hall into the X-ray cabin I could see Gita and Chintu waiting patiently. Chintu's stoic face and silence conveyed his concern.

After the X-ray, the examining doctor asked me if I had fallen somewhere, to which I said no. I couldn't recollect any incident which could even remotely resemble a fall or a slip.

While I was being taken into the MRI room after the CT scan, I told Gita and Chintu about what the doctor had said. While on the MRI table, I closed my eyes and kept clinging to the first and last hope in the sea of disbelief, discomfort and distress – Sai Baba. I prayed with all my heart and soul.

The reports didn't yield anything substantial but the last word of the doctor left me shocked. That word was 'biopsy'. Anyone who knows about the dreaded disease of cancer is aware about biopsy. Upon hearing that word, I fell into an abyss of darkness and hopelessness even though nothing had been detected so far. What cancer does at a physical level is bad, but its impact at the mental level of the patient and the family is worse. That word brought along with it the fear of the inevitable end, the corresponding pain, the harrowing experience, the turbulence of disturbing thoughts and lastly the obvious and unavoidable questions – why me, God?

I asked the doctor I could go back home and come back the following day for the biopsy. He readily agreed but with a stern caution that I shouldn't delay it. I came out of his cabin and met Gita and Chintu. I told them everything. I looked at Chintu and tried putting up a brave face, but in reality I was trying hard to hide my tears. He too couldn't look into my eyes and tried hiding his tears by attempting to hurry back home. It was only when we came back home that he broke down into uncontrollable tears. Looking at him my control gave way and I couldn't stop myself from crying. I told him that he should be strong and be the support but only a mother knows what a son, who looks up to her for everything, feels in such trying times. The day ended on a quite an emotional note but I decided to take charge of things before they took charge of me.

The next morning I had word with my dear friend Manju, who was a Deputy Director in Delhi government, and sought her advice regarding how to move forward. She correctly advised that we should take a second opinion or even a third one if required from a government hospital before we went for a biopsy. So we went to LNJP Hospital and met one of the doctors there. He suggested to do an X-ray again. Upon seeing the reports, the doctor prescribed only some physiotherapy. He asked us to visit again after a week to monitor the progress.

Every single day after that day passed very slowly. When I went to the hospital again the doctor asked me to undergo a coloured MRI to know the exact cause behind the swelling which was visible in the earlier report. On seeing the MRI reports and doing a comparative analysis with the earlier X-ray, MRI and CT Scan reports, they observed that the swelling and the white spot visible earlier had vanished. They were very surprised to see in the latest report that not even a dot was visible. A team of doctors sat together to review every possibility before they submitted their final opinion. They repeatedly asked me the reason why the earlier doctors went for so many tests. They even asked me the reason why I underwent the MRI and CT Scan when there was no requirement. I didn't have an answer and was greatly relieved when the doctors said there were no cancerous cells. I thanked them profusely for their opinion and came out of the room.

While returning Manju asked me what all I had done in the last week for my illness. I told her that I took the prescribed medicines on time and massaged the thigh area with hot mustard oil every day, as the doctor had advised. Most importantly, I woke up every morning and performed my daily rituals for Baba's pooja. I prayed sincerely asking Him to relieve me of the pain. I sought his intervention when I couldn't see any ray of hope from anywhere. I carefully followed what the doctor advised and surrendered my fate to Baba in this grim situation. No one returns empty handed from His door; I didn't either.

I thanked Manju and left for home. All through the journey, I kept wondering – Was it the medicine? Was it the prayers? I could neither ignore the expertise of the doctor who diagnosed me perfectly nor ignore the presence of the intangible source of power and hope in the world when everything in life fails.

On reaching home, I quickly unlocked the main door, went straight to the pooja room, and bowed before Baba in gratitude and humility. I couldn't control my tears of thankfulness. It seemed as if He had again conquered adversity and helped a devotee like me to recover from the mental agony of a possibility that could have devastated the lives of my near and dear ones. I sat in the pooja room for a while and read the Sai Satcharita as a token for my love towards Him and for peace of my mind.

His figure which is made of marble, shouldn't be mistaken for His silence because in reality He is omniscience and omnipresent. He listens to the devotees who place their belief and faith in him and do what they would do in normal circumstances. as per a prudent rational being. He performs His part without you knowing about it until the end. In this world of uncertainty, His abode is the confluence of endless possibilities and unadulterated faith. Om Sai Ram!

Serendipity

One of the sad truths of life is that expectations lead to disappointment. And the joy that we get from unexpected things is unmatched and unparalleled.

In 2012, I was working in the Regional Training Centre of UCO Bank, Bhubaneswar as a faculty member, busy training freshers. During March, the training centre remains shut owing to financial year closing. Having completed the assigned work, the thought of paying a visit to Shirdi struck me. The idea of seeing the silent yet engaging eyes of Baba in the Samadhi Mandir was very appealing. Before I could wake up from this dream, I had already logged into one of the travel booking websites and was looking for the available seats. Simultaneously, I called up my husband to enquire if he would accompany me. His answer left me confused because neither did he disagree with my proposal outright nor did he accept it. First, he reminded me that we had been to Shirdi couple of months earlier in January and he could consider a visit only in June during the Court vacations.

I tried diverting my mind by thinking about the upcoming faculty meet scheduled at Kolkata. Just then, I heard the Principal of the Training Centre calling me on the intercom. I answered the call, only to hear words that were music to my ears. He informed me that there was a week-long Faculty Development Programme scheduled at the National Institute of Bank Management (NIBM), Pune, which would be followed by the Faculty Meet at Kolkata. At that moment, I was transfixed upon hearing 'Pune'. I reconfirmed with him again just to be doubly sure. It felt like Baba had heard what I whispered to myself in my thoughts. What next? 'Chalo bulawa aaya hai!'

I had spoken with my co-faculty members and proposed visiting Shirdi during our visit to Pune. Happily, they agreed readily. On reaching NIBM on 14 April 2012, seven of my colleagues and I decided to go to Shirdi the following day which was a Sunday. We hired a vehicle and I started my much-awaited trip. Though I was happy that I was going to Shirdi, there was a thought that kept bothering me. Each time I went to Shirdi, I always prepared a garland of Tulsi leaves for offering at the Samadhi. On this visit I didn't find the time to make one. Nonetheless, I didn't let it dampen my spirits. I was happy about getting a chance of seeing Baba yet again – it was sheer serendipity.

Mr. Swagatam Dash, a colleague, was also a part of our group. On reaching Shirdi, he purchased a coconut, some prasad for offering and I purchased a garland. Upon coming to know that Mr. Dash was visiting Shirdi for the first time, the shopkeeper told him that the offerings should only be touched at the Baba's holy feet and taken back by the devotee. I closed my eyes and prayed to Baba, seeking forgiveness for not bringing the Tulsi garland and requesting Him to accept the garland that I had purchased. Then I put the garland in the bag that Mr. Dash was carrying and joining the serpentine queue that led to the Samadhi.

The queue moved slowly, but the religious chanting of the name of Baba takes your mind off. The moment you enter the metal railings near the Samadhi, the volunteers

Serendipity

usher you in and out of the Samadhi area at a fanatic pace. The only thing that you had been looking forward to patiently in the long queue, gets over even before you realize what happened. Anyway, the most important part was that the priest accepted Mr. Dash's offering along with my garland. We bowed to Baba and came out feeling contented. Mr. Dash took out the prasad from his bag to offer us and let out a shriek in disbelief. I still remember his words. He said, 'Madam, everything has been returned to us but except the garland.' I only smiled at him in my reply and closed my eyes to thank Baba heartily for fulfilling my wish yet again.

We returned to the NIBM campus for the week-long training. Daytimes were busy and mostly comprised training sessions by eminent trainers and faculty but evenings were relatively free. We engaged in several team-building activities which were not only fun but also a learning experience. We all went for morning and evening walks on a daily basis. During one of the morning walks, I passed by a small temple inside the campus. I thought of bringing the framed photo of Baba that I had brought from Shirdi and placing it in the temple. However, the moment I went inside I was surprised to see Baba already there. A beautiful white idol welcomed me. I paid my obeisance and left the temple with a vow that I would offer a garland to Baba that very Thursday.

I woke up early on Thursday and went out to collect flowers so that I could make the garland and offer it before the training session commenced. While roaming around to collect flowers, I came across an old lady who was also busy plucking flowers. Both of us smiled at each other. She then came forward and gestured me to open my packet. I couldn't fathom why, until she started pouring two or three handfuls of white jasmine flowers into my packet. The irony of the incident was that I didn't ask her anything and her gesture was absolutely voluntary and selfless. For working people, every minute in the morning is precious and her gesture definitely saved my time so that I could be at my training session punctually. It was Baba blessing me again! With folded hands, I thanked her and headed to my room where I could prepare the garland and offer it to Baba at the temple.

The week passed but left behind an indelible memory, a story to narrate and an experience to re-live for a lifetime. Was it mere serendipity or was it Baba who listens to my unspoken words?

I'd prefer leaving this for you to decide, because some words are best left unspoken.

Lost and Found

Baba is surely omnipotent to grant wishes of the countless folded hands seeking His attention and benevolence in numerous ways.

I clearly remember it was 12 December 2012 when my younger son Chintu had to leave for Delhi for an internship during his law school days. Because morning time office-hour was nearing when the traffic would increase, I was in a hurry to leave on time. I had already helped him pack his stuff the previous evening, arranged everything and made sure that he had packed all necessary things for his month-and-a-half long stay. I gave him ₹2,500 cash for the journey and transferred some money in his bank account. His train was scheduled to depart at 3 p.m. I wished him a comfortable journey and left for office. At around midday I received a call from him. I could sense something amiss. His voice had an uncertain tone. He told me that he had lost his wallet somewhere between the laundry shop and our home. The laundry was barely two or three hundred metres from our place and so the possibility of finding his wallet, if dropped somewhere in between, was definitely high. He said that he had searched the entire route twice and had also unpacked every bag just to be doubly sure it was not packed by mistake. Like every mother, I first asked him to leave for station on time. On the way, he should stop at the bank and take some cash from me.

I immediately blocked his ATM cards and kept a regular check on his activities lest he left late for the station and missed the train. He came to the office and I gave him the money. He was leaving with a sad face so I tried to cheer him up a little.

After returning home, I went over to the laundry to enquire about the missing wallet and if anyone had found it. The laundry person remembered that Chintu had come to look for his wallet, but nobody had reported finding it. I asked few other vendors and shopkeepers nearby who were familiar to me, but without result.

I just couldn't get the incident out of my mind because Chintu's college ID card was also in that wallet. Two days passed without any news of the missing wallet. On the third day, while I had gone to the pharmacy just opposite our home, across the main road, I happened to share the unfortunate event with the shopkeeper. His reply was pragmatic. He said that if any person had found the wallet he would have returned it in a day or two instead of keeping it with him for three days before returning it.

Just then, I recollected a small story I had read about a devotee how he was successful in finding a lost ATM card. Immediately, I retorted to the pharmacist that, if Baba was willing, anything could happen on any day. If not the money, at least the ID card and the wallet would be found.

Lo and behold! Baba overheard my conversation. The next morning my husband received a call from KIIT Law School, saying that a person had found Chintu's ID card and had contacted them using the details on it. He gave the contact number of the person so that we could get in touch with him and collect the card. My husband called me

Lost and Found

up and gave me the phone number of the person. When I called him he said he had found the wallet on the other side of the canal without any money but an ATM card and the college ID card.

Before calling Chintu to convey the news, I closed my eyes and thanked Baba from the bottom of my heart for His blessings and renewed my faith in Him.

Having shifted to Delhi in November 2014, my travelling increased considerably since I was going frequently to Bhubaneswar as well as to my elder son's place of posting. For no particular reason, I always used my passport as an identity proof during domestic travel. A friend advised me once not to do that as there was a risk of losing it. Sometime in 2016, I was heading to Bhubaneswar for a week-long stay when I decided not to use the passport for that trip. In between, I had also been to Vizag for a weekend to visit Guddu. It was a pleasant stay but like good things come to an end, so did the trip. I returned to Delhi and quickly got back into office mode. I unpacked my luggage, kept everything in its assigned place, including the passport.

Normalcy in terms of work at office resumed and I was engrossed in it completely. It was only after a week or so when I was looking for my passport that I wasn't able to find it. It seemed like my friend's words were prophetic. I searched for it everywhere. I was not even able to recollect where I had kept it after returning from Bhubaneswar. I frantically searched every single place where I could possibly have kept it, but there was no result. I informed Chintu and my maid and asked them to keep a lookout for it. Out of sheer desperation, I also enquired from my husband and Guddu, who were at Bhubaneswar and Vizag respectively. I kept searching for three long months but I could neither find my passport nor be certain that it was lost. Had I concluded that it was lost I would have started the process of making a new one.

Both my sons then cracked a joke – don't worry, your Baba will find it for you. I thought there were countless people with more serious problems in their lives who were looking to Baba with hope. Baba should be catering to them instead of looking for my passport. But I did not give up hope high of finding it. Meanwhile we had to shift from the ground floor of our apartment to the second floor. I thought to myself that this time I would surely be able to find my passport while shifting as we would be moving and shifting everything. But again I was disappointed.

Then I thought practically and applied for a new passport after lodging an FIR online for the lost passport. That same week, on Thursday, when I was doing my daily morning rituals in the pooja room, I looked at Baba's face and I thought to myself, 'Couldn't Baba do some kind of a miracle and the elusive passport comes straight into my hands?' Maybe I was putting Him to test for a trivial job. I went to office and no miracle happened on that day. I laughed at my silliness and continued doing my work.

That Sunday, I was searching for a packet of mehndi. I usually keep the packet on the top of the dressing table. The moment I put my hand there for the mehndi packet, a small, blue, leather-covered booklet came out as well. It was the passport! I let out a scream as if I had a snake in my hand. The maid came running and enquired what had happened. The moment I showed her the passport she was bewildered. She was aware about my frantic searches and she had packed every single article of the dressing table during the shifting process. She said that during the packing and shifting process, she had never seen the booklet. I laughed and asked her to continue her work.

The passport search had finally come to an end. An end which brought no reward except satisfaction because I had already applied for a new passport. Chintu had an interesting reaction to all these incidents that had been happening. He said that Baba was a one-stop solution for everything in your life, be it a lost ATM card or a lost passport.

Baba showed His Omnipotence again. Every search of mine failed until I thought of casting my burden on Him. This is a never-ending relationship of undiluted belief and faith between a devotee and the Perfect Master.

34

The Missing Crown

Those who feel I'm here at Shirdi only, have totally failed to know me because if one of my devotees is about to fall, I shall stretch my hands to support him from thousands of miles away.

These words are paraphrased from one of Baba's sayings and represent His omnipresence. We also know that He has His own myriad ways of looking after His devotees.

During November 2015, I was in Bhubaneswar for a week-long holiday on the occasion of Diwali. While at home, I prefer doing the daily pooja rituals all by myself. It gives a sense of satisfaction and happiness. I had adorned Baba's small idol with a crown. The crown not only accentuated His aesthetic appeal but also added weight to His presence among other deities. One day while performing the daily rituals I noticed that the crown on Baba's head was missing. I just couldn't accept this unusual situation and went mentally berserk. Frantically, I started looking for it in every nook and corner of the room. I didn't leave any stone unturned to find the missing crown. I enquired from my maid and my husband but couldn't get any satisfactory reply. The sight of Baba without His crown was unbearable for me. For any other person the

The Missing Crown

crown might be an ornament, but for me it was a symbol of pride. So I went to the Sai Baba Mandir at Tankapani Road and got two crowns, thinking I would use one at Bhubaneswar and the other at Delhi. I came home and placed the crown on Baba's head. That sight of Baba with his regained prominence made me feel better.

The same evening, I phoned my younger son Ishan who was in Delhi at that time. His quivering voice was ominous. He choked while talking, and I became panicky. I had tears welling up and my voice faltered. He said that he had met with a minor accident and got a cut on his forehead. I could sense his helplessness because he tends to lose consciousness and gets nauseated due to bleeding or at the sight of blood. I tried being brave and didn't allow my fears to appear in my words. He hung up saying that he was going to the doctor and would get back to me in a while. But he left me bewildered as he did not say how he met with the accident.

I was in continuous touch with him on the next day, until I boarded the flight back to Delhi. Before leaving home for any journey, it's a common custom to go to the pooja room and seek blessings. I hurriedly went up to the pooja room and was shocked at what I saw. The crown was missing again! I let out a scream of fear and disbelief. My husband and maid came running and asked me what had happened. I pointed towards Baba's head and said that the crown that I had placed the day earlier was missing. They said that it might have been taken away by some mice or rat or could have been misplaced. I didn't agree with them. Even though the crown was a little loose, it couldn't have fallen off His head on the ground and gone missing. Without losing any more time, I took out the second crown that I had thought of using in Delhi and placed it on Baba. During the entire journey to the airport, my mind was full of questions for which I didn't have any answer.

I reached Delhi in the morning and headed straight to office with my luggage. I came back home in the evening, left my luggage in the hallway and went directly to the pooja room. I bowed to Baba and when I got up I saw something completely unbelievable. The crown on Baba's forehead was missing here in Delhi as well. I was speechless and couldn't understand about the similarity of events at two different places.

Meanwhile Chintu came back from office. I made him sit down and first inspected the injury. The cut was quite deep, almost an inch in size, on the forehead. When I asked him, he narrated the details of the incident. He said that he was riding his bicycle when he grazed the side of a protruding, partially cut branch of a tree, which had been cut recently. This was just before the traffic signal. The area was unlit and in the darkness he couldn't see the branch. He came back to the house with his bleeding forehead and was in great pain, almost at the cusp of unconsciousness, when he received that call from me which made him alert and go to the doctor. In my mind, I thanked Baba for his blessings.

It was only then I asked him about Baba's missing crown. He said that the crown had fallen off and the maid had found it. If he had put it on Baba again, it would have fallen off again. So he had kept it safely. We went into the pooja room and the crown was where he had kept it.

The entire night there were many questions in my head. It could not be a mere coincidence that the same event occurred at the same time at two different places. When I had spoken to my husband and my elder son earlier, neither had a convincing explanation. I felt there was something in the events which needed to be interpreted, which is not yet clear to us. Someone was beckoning me to see the unseen, hear the unheard and comprehend the incomprehensible. Someone was trying to guide me through this path.

The Missing Crown

Despite the disturbed night I woke up early morning for my walk and decided to visit the place where Chintu had met with the accident. I was shocked to see the partially cut branch. It was 25 to 30 inches wide and very sharp at the edges. The branch was protruding from a tree growing on the footpath that was tilting towards the road. For a moment I could imagine how fatal the accident could have been if Chintu had hit the centre of the branch instead of the side. He just missed it by a few inches. A chill run down my spine. I thanked Baba again when I realized that Chintu had a narrow escape from a more fatal injury.

I was slowly walking back home when I started joining the dots. Gradually, the answers appeared. Baba had been trying to communicate with me and inform me about a lurking danger that was hovering over my family. It was only because of His grace that Chintu was safe with only a small injury. Tears started rolling down my eyes in relief and gratitude.

I reached home and bowed down before Baba, thanking Him for keeping my family safe. This was one of His numerous actions which increase the faith and trust of His devotees. I called up my husband and elder son and narrated them the entire story of Baba's miracle. They agreed. Meanwhile Chintu, though half asleep, had been listening to my conversation. Later when I left for office, he texted me, 'Mama, does your Baba communicate everything with you?' I replied, 'Yes, He does, if one surrenders oneself completely to Him.'

I sat for a while closed my eyes and asked Baba, 'Why do you love me so much?' I didn't get an answer because I know He would be busy somewhere answering yet another distress call from one of His devotees.

One who believes is already blind in His love, and for one who doesn't, it is only a step away from being in His love.

35

You Have One Unread Message

In the realm of Baba, without His grace, not a single leaf can move. It is His will that decides the fate of we mortals. If it had not been for Baba, I wouldn't have been able to visit Shirdi so many times. In fact, I have spent three new year mid nights at Shirdi along with my husband.

Having shifted to Delhi in November 2014 after a job transfer, spending the New Year eve in Shirdi was not possible. Somehow from the first day of 2015, I had a strong desire to visit Shirdi as soon as possible. Then I found a perfect window for my visit. There was a continuous stretch of holidays from 1 April to 4 April. Having firmly decided to visit Shirdi at that time, suddenly I started visualizing the Samadhi Mandir. Maybe this was His act of beckoning His devotee. I called up my husband and shared my plan with him. Owing to his busy schedule he expressed his inability to come. He suggested that I could take some friends from Delhi with me. Then I asked Chintu if he would like to accompany me but his reply was on the same lines as his father. Their suggestion left me confused because I had shifted to Delhi only two months earlier and so I didn't have many close friends yet. Nevertheless, I listened to my Master's call and booked the tickets to Shirdi alone. Then began the endless wait until the time I boarded my flight and the set foot on the holy land of Shirdi. This waiting is always filled with a lot of excitement about visiting Shirdi yet again as well the anxiety of not doing or missing out the necessary rituals there.

I had never visited Shirdi empty handed. I always carried some homemade ladoos and a garland of Tulsi leaves for Baba. This time I was feeling a little awkward as I had not been able to find the place from where I could get enough Tulsi leaves for the garland. I mentioned this to Manju, and old friend who has been in Delhi for 30 years. She was working as a Deputy Director with the Delhi Government at that time. She said she would arrange the Tulsi leaves.

A as the date of the journey approached, a feeling of doubt came in me. It started to dilute the courage with which I had booked the tickets and decided to undertake the journey all alone. A fear of unknown that made rethink my decision each time I thought about it. Adding to my hesitation were Chintu's repeated words, 'Mama, don't go alone. Take someone along with you.' But with whom could I go? Meanwhile, Manju had called a couple of times to confirm the date of my travel so that she could provide me the Tulsi leaves on time.

Three days before the journey, I sprained my ankle while walking on the road. I was disheartened because the injury could force me to cancel my visit to Shirdi. I remember I came back home and slumped into the couch, holding my swollen ankle with one hand and asked Baba, 'Why did you do this to me? 'How do you think I'll be able to go to Shirdi with this injured foot?' I applied some gel rested the injured ankle by propping it against a pillow. I kept my morale high and decided to visit a doctor the next morning. Surprisingly, when I woke up the next morning the ankle didn't pain or feel stiff. It was as if nothing had happened to it. I suppose He was listening to my cries and arranged the miraculous cure. Strange, but true!

Then I got a call from my friend Smita, who informed me that she was going to Shirdi on 2 April, though her route and timings were different. We would meet at Shirdi. I was happy that a familiar face and like-minded company would be there. The feeling of being alone on the trip started to fade away. Then my brother-in-law called and said that he and seven other devotees would be going to Shirdi on 3 April and he would meet me there. Suddenly, from no one, I had the company of so many people. This was yet another of His miracles for His devotee. Believe it or not!

The first day of April was a holiday for us, so I decided to maximize the use of the available time. Early morning I sorted and arranged every essential thing that was required in the course of my journey and also in Shirdi for my rituals. At around 9 a.m. Manju called me and said that she was sending the Tulsi leaves. Once we hung up, I wondered why a lady, who was so sincere about trying to get me Tulsi leaves, couldn't come on the trip as well? Her office was also closed during these days. I called and asked her, 'Why don't you accompany me to Shirdi?' All this while she had been under the assumption that I was going with my husband. When I said that I was going alone, she said she was happy to consider the idea of going to Shirdi. She asked for a little time to confirm as she had to attend some guests at home.

I waited eagerly for her call. After some time she called and said she would be able to go to Shirdi, but she was able to get the flight booking from Delhi to Pune in the evening flight and not the morning one in which I was going. She was not sure if she should go ahead with the booking. I told her to go ahead, as I could wait for her at Pune airport till her flight arrived. I was very happy. There was no feeling of being alone any more, rather it was a sense of security and safety. Baba had blessed me again.

The next morning I took a cab for the airport. With nothing else to do, I open my bag to check my phone. The

You Have One Unread Message

screen said, 'You have one unread message.' It was a text from Manju. She said that her flight was not for the evening but in the morning, just fifteen minutes after my flight. She hadn't seen the time properly earlier. With happiness and disbelief, I had tears of joy while I kept reading the text happily again and again. I recollected what Baba said – There is no need to fear when He was there. I went into a state of trance and could hear the voice whispering into my ears saying, 'My child, why are you afraid of the loneliness when you're coming to me. It's my sole responsibility of taking care of you. Now that everything has been secured for you, just come to my home.' The cab came to a halt and I stepped out to His calling.

Manju and I met at the Pune airport. It was Baba's day, that is, Thursday.

We had a satisfying visit. I placed a lit diya at Lendibagh and prepared a Rangoli. The security guard at Lendibagh smiled at me upon seeing the big diya and my devotion while making the Rangoli. He remarked, 'Aap kariye, hum hain na.' (You continue doing your thing, I'm here). I felt as if the security guard was speaking Baba's words and assuring me of my well-being there.

During our trip we visited Ellora and Ajanta Caves as well as the Jyotirlingam at Ghrishneshwar and Trimbakeshwar. We ensured that we took part in the devout Kaakad and Seja Aarti of Baba.

From a journey that wasn't materializing to an experience which was mesmerizing, this was wonderful. Obviously, there is that invisible and supernatural power that smoothens creases of fate and straightens the crooked paths of life. You may call it Rama or Jesus or Allah, I have known Him as Baba.

36

Happy New Year

From 2011 to 2013 I had been spending my New Years, along with my husband, at Shirdi. This had become a regular custom for me. To ensure that it was not broken, I planned for the visit of December 2013 early, during the year itself. By His grace the tickets were booked and reservations for lodging were done for two days each at Dwarabati and the UCO Bank Holiday Home. Irrespective of the number of times I have visited earlier, the excitement that builds up before each trip is unchanged even now. It seems like my closeness to Baba keeps the child in me alive.

This time I had made up a mental list of the rituals that I wished to perform at Shirdi – Sai Abhishek Pooja, Sai Satyabrat Pooja, Aarti and so on. In order to ensure that everything happened smoothly, I started arranging for all the necessary materials that would be required for performing the rituals. I also got myself a big diya, cotton wick, ghee and incense sticks to be lit at Lendibagh and some coloured powder to make Rangoli there as well.

Visiting Shirdi empty handed makes me feel incomplete; I feel hollow from within. So each time I go, I always make some ladoos and a garland of Tulsi leaves for Baba. Offering Him anything that I have made myself gives me a feeling of immense satisfaction. I feel as if I have given Him the

Happy New Year

best of myself with a vow to return with something better. I prepared the Tulsi leaves garland along with the ladoos of Suji, Khajur and Gur. I remember making around 25 to 30 ladoos for offering. During the preparations time I kept telling Baba, 'I have prepared this with a sincere heart, full of love, so it's Your turn now how You accept it.'

We reached Shirdi on the morning of 31 December. We had a quick shower and rushed to the Samadhi Mandir with our handbags full of our offerings. We joined the serpentine queue that leads to the darshan. Crowds of devotees had thronged Shirdi to begin the new year in the lap of Baba's blessings. The air was overflowing with devotion towards Baba. Despite carrying so many bags, I kept my pace with the queue. My husband was concerned how I would be able to offer all that I had brought along with me in that rush. So he stood behind me and kept pushing me to the front lest I miss the coveted chance for any reason. Though I was acting as per his instructions, I was totally silent, anxious in the prevailing confusion, looking at the overpowering crowd that was multiplying every second. Instead of breaking down, I did what I knew best. I repeated my prayer to Baba, asking Him to take care of me and accept my offerings for Him, now that I was there at His doorstep.

We moved slowly with the queue until the prized moment came. We reached the Samadhi and the spot adjacent to Baba's idol. First, I handed over the bag which had the Tulsi garland in it. I remember when the priest took out the garland from the bag, he looked at me, being shocked seeing the length of the garland. He spread it over Baba's Samadhi. First offering.☐

The massive rush was maddening, with people packed so closely that it was difficult to even move my hands. With much difficulty, I pulled out my second bag containing the ladoos and handed it over to the priest. He took the bag and touched it at the Baba's lotus feet. He had turned around to hand over the bag back to me when all of a sudden, he sat down and opened it. He took out the ladoos and I very vividly remember that he offered nine ladoos to Baba, one by one. With eyes wide open and mouth agape, my husband and I were both stunned at what we were witnessing in front of us. I had tears of joy standing before my Master. It was a moment which bound me to Baba stronger than before. I wish I could have captured the moment in a more substantial and tangible way instead of just storing it in my memory and re-living it time and again. I still don't know why the priest sat down with the bag when he had already turned around and almost given it back to me. Amidst all the rush and melee that day, Baba heard my prayers and accepted what was always meant for Him only. Second offering.

The priest returned the bag of ladoos to us and we got an opportunity to be in the central hall of the Samadhi Mandir from where one can look at Baba's idol directly. We prostrated in the hall before Baba and thanked Him for his enduring love and kindness towards us. After being there for 10–15 minutes, we left the Samadhi Mandir.

We paid a visit to Dwarkamayi and Gurusthan along with the Hanuman, Shiva and Ganesha Mandir located there. Then I proceeded to Lendibagh where a group of devotees from Andhra Pradesh were already busy decorating the place with Rangoli and small earthen lamps. Seeing their enthusiasm, I took out the big diya I had been carrying all along with me from home for this revered moment. I got it ready for lighting and placed ghee, camphor and cotton wick in it. The group of devotees happily came over and we planned to place the big diya at the centre of their Rangoli. In unison and with a loudly resonating chant of 'Sai Ram', we placed the diya at the centre of the Rangoli.

We were in Shirdi until 4 January so my husband and I made a conscious effort to visit the temple a number of times. We saw that my diya continued to be at its place, and hadn't been moved. Each time we came to call on Baba we went to Lendibagh to check on it. Every time there was someone or the other who was refilling the diya with some ghee and camphor. The sight of the earthen

Happy New Year

lamp burning brightly became a matter of happiness and satisfaction for me. It made me believe that Baba doesn't overlook the sincerity and dedication of His devotees. This time also during our stay, we performed the Sai Abhishek and Sai Satyabrat Pooja. I even completed the parayan with the holy Sai Satcharita within a span of three days on the hallowed soil of Shirdi.

On the last day of our stay, I wished to visit Kopargaon. I had read that Baba had been visiting that place. A Sai devotee, who also happened to be hailing from Odisha, explained the relevance of Kopargaon to me.

We went to the 'Corner Temple' at Kopargaon situated on the bank of Godavari river. It was the place where Baba had first come, meditated and stayed before moving to Shirdi. Upon visiting the temple, I got to know its name – Shri Saibaba Tapobhumi Mandir. I felt like sitting there for a long time and soaking myself in the religious atmosphere of the place located in the lap of nature but couldn't do that owing to the limited time.

I returned not only satisfied and happy but also aware about so many things related to Baba. While on my return journey I was checking my phone when I saw few messages. I opened the first one and it read, 'Wishing you a prosperous and happy new year.' Indeed, it was a very happy new year!

Baba listens to those who are true in their ways. He listens to those who surrender themselves completely before Him. He listens to those who are His and He is theirs. Devotion is a two-way traffic where the outgoing route is definitely crowded but the incoming route may be absolutely silent and strange. This silence is nothing but His omniscience and the strangeness is nothing but the countless ways in which He caters to His devotees.

37
Service Before Self

As social beings, humans learn from the society to evolve as informed and better beings. Therefore, it is our moral duty to give something back to the society in any form, shape, size or kind. It is the intent that counts and not the form. Thus, the first and foremost rule of rendering any kind of service is to ensure that our personal interests take a back seat and the recipients' interests are paramount.

Nothing makes me happier than the sight of a person selflessly working for the betterment of the community or rendering some kind of service to others. During 2009-2011, when I regularly visited the Sai Baba Temple at Tankapani road, I always used to see Smita's mother, Mrs. Panda, even at the age of 70, deeply engrossed in some work or the other. It was rare to see her standing still. Her active lifestyle defied the stereotypes attached to septuagenarians. You could see her arranging the books in the Parayan Hall or assisting the devotees to move in a queue or distributing prasad to the devotees. Given the fact that Smita and I were in college together, she had known me since then. I looked up to her as a mother figure and she reciprocated my regard for her with love and care.

Service Before Self

One day during my visit to the temple, I found Mrs. Panda deeply involved with some work. I went up to her, touched her feet and sought her blessings. She was happy to see me and asked me about my well-being. I asked her if I could join her or do some other work as a service for Baba. She told me not to bother as I was busy with my office, home and family as of then. She said that anyone who believes and has submitted to Baba's devotion will be called for service at the right time. That opportunity to give back to the society in His name is solely His call. It will come. I took her leave but had an uncertain and mixed feelings about her reply. I was anxious of getting that call and the happiness of being one amongst the numerous who have been chosen by Baba to render some form of service.

That evening, during my usual visit to the temple, I saw a small crowd in front of the Parayan Hall. When I went forward to enquire, I saw a senior devotee, Mr. P.C. Mishra, was busy explaining something to the people there. From a distance, I could not understand what he was saying. After the crowd dispersed, I went up to Mr. Mishra and asked him what the matter was. He told me that they were planning to send a representation to the railway department to start a special train from Bhubaneswar to Shirdi and in order to send the letter, he required around one hundred signatures of devotees. Without a minimum number of signatures the proposal would not be considered. I immediately signed the letter. The person sitting on the other side of the table told Mr. Mishra that I was working with UCO Bank and was a regular visitor at the temple.

After some time, Mr. Mishra asked me whether I had read his article in the monthly magazine about Baba's miracles. Before I could answer him, a group of devotees came up to enquire what we were doing. I just couldn't keep quiet and explained about the proposal and the necessity of their signatures. The devotees were convinced with my explanation and signed the application.

Soon many small groups of devotees came over to us. On seeing that I had taken the lead to explain to them, Mr. Mishra took a break saying that he had a back pain. He said he would take a walk and would be back quickly. I continued to do my work. Actually, I was enjoying being involved in the work for Baba.

There was a regular stream of devotees at our desk. I explained to them the issues and answered their questions patiently. They were happy to sign on the application and with each signature, my confidence increased. Some devotees were so happy with the proposal that they asked me for my phone number so that they could check about the status of the train. Without any prior planning, I had got involved in a job that was related to Baba. I was very happy about it.

After an hour or so Mr. Mishra came back and enquired about the number of signatures that had been collected by then. When I counted, the figure was an astonishing 115. We had surpassed the minimum numbers required. He was very happy about my work and at the same time was surprised about the large number of signatures.

He mentioned his article in the monthly magazine about Baba's miracles again. He also asked me if I had experienced any miracles ever. I smiled at him and told him that all that happened now was more a miracle because he had left with exactly 12 signatures on the paper, which reached 115 in an hour, and just a little while earlier I had begged for some work. I thanked him for giving me an opportunity to serve the cause of Baba. I left the temple with a wide smile and a content heart.

Since my college days I have been actively involved in blood donation camps. I have been an active donor since then. I have been fortunate enough to have donated blood thrice under the patronage of Baba in the blood donation camps organized by Sai Baba Mandir, Tankapani and Dattatreya Sai Mandir Dhenkanal.

Service Before Self

I will always remember 2 November 2014 as an eventful day in my life. That was the day when I left my home to fly to Delhi for joining CERSAI, Ministry of Financial Services, on deputation. The day is also embedded deeply in my memory because of the service I rendered in the name of Baba before boarding that life-changing flight to Delhi.

Two days before my travel date, I went to the Sai Baba temple at Jay Durga Nagar, where I saw a notice about a blood donation camp on 2 November at 10 a.m. Without giving any thought, I firmly decided to donate blood first, and then leave for my flight.

On that day, I reached the temple by 9 a.m. and completed my darshan quickly to join the queue for the blood donation. Many of the volunteers who were managing the camp knew me because of my frequent visits to the temple. They also knew about my transfer to Delhi. I requested them to allow me to donate blood a little early as I had a flight to catch later. They were happy to help and got me ahead in the queue. After the donation, I had some refreshments and took rest for a while before thinking of hurrying back home.

While resting, I could overhear a few volunteers talking amongst themselves. They required someone with a good handwriting so that they could have the certificates filled neatly before giving them to the donors. Suddenly, one of the volunteers remarked that since I worked at a bank, I must have a good handwriting, so I could fill the certificates. I couldn't say no to that enthusiastic group of volunteers.

I quickly got busy filling the certificates. I was so deeply involved in the work that I didn't keep a track of the time. Finally, when I looked at my watch, it was nearly 1 p.m. I had to leave home at least by 4 p.m. for the 6 p.m. flight. I wound up the work immediately and took permission from the organizers and volunteers to leave. I had completed 48 certificates by that time. They thanked me profusely for my assistance and I smiled back at them with a deep sense of fulfilment.

Before leaving I went up few steps just to have another look at Baba's face. When I looked at Him, I felt as if He was smiling at me. I folded my hands and bowed before him. I walked down the stairs with a large smile on my face. While going back home I could hear the familiar voice of my Master telling me, 'You had asked me to give you an opportunity to render some service. March ahead and serve as many as you can.'

The world would definitely become a better place to live, with a lot more peace and harmony amongst us if we keep 'them' before 'us' and 'you' before 'me'. All the world requires is a little more love and care.

38

Last-In First-Out

The chain of miraculous experiences started from the day I stepped into the world of Baba. These experiences weren't one-off occurrences but rather continual in nature. Every experience was distinct and was different from the preceding one. This kept me intrigued and thrilled at the same time, because I always wondered, 'What's next?'

My first step in the world of Baba had been solely influenced by my friend, Smita. Had it not been for her, I wouldn't have experienced this divine pleasure. Be it the phone calls when she used to discuss with me at length about Baba and His miraculous world or her endless invitations for me to take part in Sai Abhishek Pooja and the various Aartis, etc., her encouragement was endless. Owing to my hectic schedule at work and preoccupation with my family, I couldn't attend all the events for which she invited me. It was her persistence that made me love Baba as I do today.

I developed an interest and affinity towards Baba just by listening to what Smita used to tell me. It was as if she was introducing me to one of her friends over a period of time, slowly and steadily. This interest pushed me to learn more about Baba through books, magazines and anything relating to Baba that I could lay my hand on. Reading about Him initiated an eagerness to look forward to reading in the various magazines available about miracles from a devotee's perspective. When I slowly entered the world of Baba, I also experienced many miracles. I started sharing them with Smita whenever we spoke. During those conversations, I remember she told me to keep a note of all these experiences by writing them down somewhere lest I forget them with time. Writing such experiences only amplifies the presence of Baba and nurtures a sense of belief about Him amongst other people.

Her suggestion opened up a new dimension of engagement in my life. I tried writing down my experiences, but something or the other stalled the process, bringing it to an abrupt end. In fact, now when I am writing this book, I think I wasn't able to do this earlier because His calling had not been there. Once I started writing about my experience, I became interested to get it published. To get an idea about submission of manuscript and subsequent publication, I spoke to Mr. Satya Khadagray, editor of *Sai Nirmalaya*. I asked him how much time it took to get a manuscript published after submission. His answer didn't satisfy an impatient soul like me. He said normally the time involved was 3-4 months, provided the writing was up to their submission standards, but it also depended upon backlog of pending work.

During December 2012, the interviews for Institute of Banking Personnel Selection (IBPS) were scheduled to be held at our bank's training college and I had been assigned the job of verifying the documents of the candidates. The timings for us were 8 a.m. to 8 p.m., but my work was over by 3 p.m. However, we were required to be present until the end as we were administrating the smooth conduct of the interviews. So we had to wait until the Interview Board finished their work for the day.

Last-In First-Out

I couldn't just sit idle for the next couple of hours doing absolutely nothing, so I decided to use the time to start writing my experiences with Baba. Before starting, I closed my eyes and prayed to Baba to guide me in my work and give me the strength to finish it. Luckily, the first story was completed the same evening, without any hiccups. Upon reaching home, I was feeling pretty happy and refreshed, so I decided to pay a visit to the Sai Baba Mandir at Jay Durga Nagar. After a nice darshan, just when I was about to start for home, I saw a notice which called for submission of articles for publication in the magazine *Sai Kripa*. I was speechless. The coincidence was tremendous. I had just finished my first story and there was a call for publication right in front of my eyes. It felt like a blessing from Baba to go ahead with what I had started. I was happy with feeling that Baba kept an eye over me. The next day itself I submitted my story to the temple trust for publication. It was published in the first edition of *Sai Kripa* in February 2013.

At that time, I wrote about another experience 'Note Counting Service at Shirdi'. I kept the copy of the article in a sealed envelope addressed to the office of *Sai Nirmalaya* at Cuttack, Odisha and gave it to the dispatch desk of my office. Then I got busy with my work. After a few days when I checked, I was disappointed to find the envelope still lying there. I requested the dispatch person to post it as soon as possible. That was on 31 January.

A day prior to Valentine's day, on 13 February, I received a call from a girl who was also a Sai devotee and knew me well. She said she was very happy when she saw my article and immediately called me to congratulate. I thanked her with all humility for her sweet gesture and encouraged her to start writing as well. All this while I was under the assumption that the article she was referring to was the one published in the February edition of *Sai Kripa*. It was only when she said that she had read it in *Sai Nirmalaya* about the note counting story that I was filled with excitement. But I wondered how it was possible. Just to be sure I checked with her again – if it was *Sai Kripa* or *Sai Nirmalaya*. The latter was the oldest running Odia magazine which published such stories and anecdotes from Sai devotees while the former was a new magazine that was started recently by the Trust of Sai Baba Temple at Jay Durga Nagar. When she confirmed that it was indeed *Sai Nirmalaya*, I didn't know whether it was a case of mistaken publication or one of Baba's miracles. The editor of *Sai Nirmalaya* had clearly told me that for an article to be published, it took 3-4 months provided it met their submission standards and also depended on the pending back-log. My article was sent on the last day of January so it should have been published in April or May. From the date of dispatch to the date of that phone call, it had only been a fortnight, which meant the article was received, vetted and published within the first week of February itself.

I sat in my chair and my eyes glistened with tears of gratitude for Baba. I tried to reconcile an unlikely though welcome event with the happiness of succeeding at something like that. Now when I think about, I strongly feel that had it not been His divine intervention, the article couldn't have been published so swiftly. While I was speculating on a whirlpool of permutation and combinations, I knew somewhere He was watching over me, observing every single action of mine and listening to every single prayer.

It is only the manifestation of His will and directions that we mortals are blessed every single time we wish for something. Just another thought – Don't you think if all our wishes came true, all the temples, churches and mosques would be empty?

Sai-Chology

At times rational beings like us should let go our scepticism so that we can see the presence of the Almighty – a presence that is fuelled by belief and faith. At times needlessly questioning the happening of an event is only due to our inability to acknowledge His actions. The Almighty can only be seen from the eyes of a believer, because only belief can show the visibility in the invisibility of the invincible.

I have worked my entire life in UCO Bank and it shall be where I retire from. Sometimes the chance to work in some other organization on deputation becomes available and the opportunity is intimated through bank notifications. One such notification was circulated in 2014 for two posts – Debt Recovery Tribunal (DRT) and Central Registry of Securitisation Asset Reconstruction and Security Interest (CERSAI). At that time I was a faculty in the Regional Training College of UCO Bank at Ashoka Market, Bhubaneswar. My interest to apply for the posts stemmed from the fact that I had not got through one of my Scale-4 promotion interviews. Though I had never thought of leaving the comforts of my home on account of deputation, I still went ahead and applied for the positions. A small reason behind this was also that my younger son had been working in Delhi since June 2013 and this interview was to be held in Delhi. So it was the perfect pretext to meet him.

I applied for the posts in the normal course. After a few months I got to know that my candidature had been rejected for the post in DRT due to technical grounds. The status of my application to CERSAI was still unknown. Meanwhile, I kept myself busy with my usual work at office and did not lose hope of getting a call for an interview for the CERSAI position.

On 15 September 2014, when I was on my way back home, I got a call from the Principal of my RTC. He informed me that I had been shortlisted for a personal interview for CERSAI. The interview was on 22 September. I was happy and excited on getting the news and shared it with my family members. Somehow, the Principal of RTC, who came from Delhi, wasn't very pleased about my interview as my selection there could disrupt the well-settled and established working of our training college. He wasn't keen to dispense with my services as a faculty member.

I went for my interview at Delhi, which went much better than what I had visualized. It was the words of the Chairman of the Interview Board that made me realize that I had been selected on the spot. He asked me, 'Madam, when are you coming to join here?' I was elated upon hearing his words. At the same time I had apprehensions about moving so far away from home. When I shared the news with my husband, he wholeheartedly supported me to work for achievement of professional goals and encouraged me to move to Delhi. Rather, he eased the situation and asked – if it had been a transfer on the grounds of longest stay in the zone (we are supposed to be transferred periodically), what would have been my decision? I would have had to accept the transfer. In the same manner, this deputation to CERSAI Delhi should be accepted as a challenge.

Then I called my elder son and gave him the news. His reply left me with a sense of confidence and security. Guddu said he was confident of my selection because the name of this organization – CERSAI – had a SAI in it. I laughed at his wit, but his words left an imprint on my mind. They bolstered my confidence and encouraged me to go ahead.

Finally, everything was set for the big move and I left Bhubaneswar on 1 November 2014. The unfamiliarity of a new place brings along a lot of excitement but also second thoughts and apprehensions. I wondered how I would manage to settle in a new city all alone and how I would fare professionally. I also kept thinking how I would be able to meet Baba whenever I wished. The strength of one's character only flourishes during an adversity or challenge. This was a challenge that I had taken up and had to live up to it, come what may. And in such situations the best help that we can get is from our Master or Guide or Lord. Luckily, my faith and belief, which was also my strength, was with me every second, all the time.

In Delhi, I was put up at Odisha Sadan, which was the guest house of the Odisha State Government, while searching for a place to shift. My first day at CERSAI was nothing short of a story from the book of Baba's miraculous experiences. I reached office, introduced myself and exchanged pleasantries with all my colleagues present there. I was directed to my seat where I was welcomed by none other than my very own Baba. The previous officer had kept a lovely idol of Baba on the desk. I smiled happily looking at Baba's idol on my new office table. It was His fortuitous, pleasing and satisfying presence on my arrival that gave me an indication about the brightness of my forthcoming days there.

Around 5 p.m. I got a call from one of my old friends, Gita, Capt. Sarada Das's wife. She gave me a pleasant surprise by arriving at my office at Bhikaji Cama Place and asked me to finish my work quickly and accompany her. It was my first day, so there wasn't any work as such for me except completion of joining formalities, which were almost done.

I walked towards her car without asking where we were going. The car started and we got busy talking. Only after some time did I come to know that we were going to the Sai Baba Temple and Jagannath Mandir at Hauz Khas. We first stopped at the temple on August Kranti road to pay our obeisance to Baba there. Once we got back into the car to proceed to the Jagannath Mandir, I got to know that Gita and her family were ardent devotees of Baba as well. So my first day at CERSAI ended with multiple darshans of Baba.

After the darshan, she dropped me at Odisha Sadan and went back home. In the evening I spoke to Capt. Sarada, Gita's husband, and requested him to help me in finding a place to stay in Delhi. He suggested I should consider staying near their house, which was in Dwarka, so that we could support each other in case of any emergency. I was happy to agree to his suggestion.

The following day Capt. Sarada took me to a property broker. The broker showed three flats out of which one was not within my budget, one wasn't well ventilated but the last one met my requirements perfectly. It was located on the main road, and quite near the airport. There was a market just behind the apartment complex, within walking distance. But it wasn't just the comfort of these facilities that made me choose Sahara Apartments. The main reason was because I felt Baba wanted me to. When the broker took me to show this flat, workers were busy painting and repairing the place. But what caught my attention is the large calendar of Baba that was hanging on one of the walls. Was it a mere coincidence that the workers had not pulled it down yet to clean the walls? Or was Baba, by His presence, telling me to stay there? Whatever it was, at that very moment I decided that I would stay there and for me this place would become *Sai Ka Sahara*.

The subsequent shifting and setting up the place were never a challenge as Gita was a blessing in all ways. From arranging for the Griha Pravesh pooja to ensuring that even the holes for the nails which were required to hang various things were drilled properly, she did everything. Had she not been there, it would have been very difficult for me. Thanks to her patience and hard work, it became a pleasant experience and eventually a bright and happy memory.

The unfamiliar city of Delhi slowly acquired a warm and congenial, home-like atmosphere. The presence of people with the same belief and faith like Gita and her family were signs of His presence and blessings. Baba ensured that I did not feel lonely by sending one of His favourite children, Gita, to be with me. She not only helped me in settling down comfortably in Delhi, but also created a real home away from home for me.

Soon Chintu, who was in Delhi before my arrival because of his job, shifted with me and the place started to radiate the ambiances of a home, a home that I could call *mine*. I remember, when my husband came to Delhi during Christmas vacations, he was surprised to see the setup of my house. He remarked that the transition from a house to your home has definitely been great. I nodded to him and whispered to myself, 'Yes indeed, my Baba.'

Now when I sit down and look back, I find that Baba held my hand from the beginning itself, at every step. He ensured His presence directly or indirectly through His disciples, and never left me alone, lest I felt lonesome and got lost in the maze of this new place. For some people, the chain of these events might have an alternate interpretation, but I know for sure that it's His omnipresence that is always looking after me, even while I'm writing all this. My belief and faith in Him defines my psychology or SAI-CHOLOGY as I call it. How about you?

40

The Light at the End of the Tunnel

Shirdi Sai Baba says, 'I have my eyes on those who love me.'

I always find substance and meaning in these words because over all these years, Baba has kept an eye on my family and me from close quarters just like a guardian. The fact is that I never asked for much from Him while I always believed He gave something extra whenever I received anything from Him. The foundation of this relationship is simply reposing my faith completely in Him and unquestionably surrendering to Him.

I had appeared for a promotion interview for the post of Senior Manager on 4 May 2011. A fortnight later there was a notification which invited applications for faculty members at the Regional Training College (RTC). I had always been keen to become a faculty and cater to my academic side. Teaching and grooming youngsters is not only challenging but also immensely satisfying. Their future is moulded as a result of your labour and efforts. It's like nurturing a sapling into a full-grown plant. The deadline for the application was 23 May. Due to the pressure of work and preoccupation with household affairs, I forgot

The Light at the End of the Tunnel

to submit my application by the stipulated deadline. Two days after the deadline had passed, I mentioned this to my colleagues. Even though I was feeling a little sad, I looked at an old man standing before one of the counters in the branch. Looking at him I realized that maybe, by serving these senior citizens and people in this rural area, I was achieving a bigger goal. I felt satisfied but not contented because I had messed up a little. Indeed, to err is human!

After a short while, I got a call from an unknown number. Presuming it to be a loan defaulter from the village or some senior citizen, I answered the phone call. What I heard from the other end was incredible. The caller was a lady who came straight to the point and asked, 'Madam, are you interested in the post of Faculty?' I immediately said yes and asked her how she came to know I was interested. Her answer made light of the matter which was a big issue in my head. She said, 'Just like that.' That didn't appear believable. I told her I had missed the deadline to apply. She replied immediately, 'Precisely, that is why I have called you. The number of applications received for the post of faculty members is less, so the deadline for submission has been extended. Please apply directly to the head-office and also mark a copy to the zonal office.' I thanked her profusely for her timely intimation and requested her for an application form as I did not have it. She said she was at the Government Secretariat Branch and I could collect the form from her.

The lady who called me was our Purnima Ma'am. Both of us had worked together for a few days at the Government Secretariat Branch just before my posting to Balakati Branch. But we hadn't exchanged contact numbers.

Upon reaching the Government Secretariat Branch, Purnima Ma'am gave me two applications forms, arranged for a table and chair where I could comfortably sit and fill them, and ordered a cup of tea for me too. Before continuing with her work, she told me to post the applications that day itself via speed post. I quickly filled the forms between sips of tea. After finishing the first form, I thought the second one was only a copy. But surprisingly, it wasn't. They were two separate forms, one for the post of General Faculty and the other for Core Banking Solution (CBS) Faculty. I thought to myself that it would be a perfect excuse to get a break from the monotony of office work by going to Kolkata for appearing in both the interviews. So I filled the second form also and dispatched both the forms immediately. Before leaving the branch, I told Purnima Ma'am my reason for filling both the forms and we had a hearty laugh. She said that she had applied for the post of General Faculty only and that I would get selected for the CBS Faculty position owing to my rich experience in that domain. I thanked her for the timely help and hospitality and took her leave.

On 30 June I received the news of my promotion to Senior Manager. Obviously, I was very happy. But before I could start celebrating, Head Office informed that I had been transferred to the Sambalpur Branch and that I should be relieved from my current branch, that is, Balakati, by 16 July. Thus, I had to finish the pending work at my branch quickly and complete the handover process. There was no news about my application for the Faculty posts. I was alternating between happiness at my promotion and anxiety about the challenging transfer. I had not left the vicinity of Bhubaneswar so far. Bhubaneswar was not just a hometown but rather a habit that I had got used to in all these years. The feeling of leaving the place soon wasn't great. I felt I was enveloped by a mass of dark clouds all over.

The first news about the Faculty position came for the post of General Faculty. I had not been shortlisted. I was disappointed as I met all the requirements of the post. I felt like I was going down an abyss of rejection and disappointment. But as they say, nothing is permanent, neither darkness nor sorrow. That evening itself, the Zonal Office called and said I had been shortlisted for the post of CBS Faculty. In fact, I was at the top of the list of all the shortlisted candidates. Suddenly I could see a small light at the end of the dark tunnel. But there was still a lot to do.

My interview was scheduled from 9 to 11 July in Kolkata. There was a challenge as I had to give a presentation using PowerPoint slides. My knowledge of computers is fair, but I had not used PowerPoint earlier. Anyway, I learned the basics quickly, prepared the PowerPoint presentation and appeared for the interview. I remember my anxiety levels were making me feel slight feverish. Thankfully, the interview went well. I was very happy when, at the end of the interview, the General Manager remarked, 'Excellent!' The Kolkata visit came to an end and I headed back home as I had to be relieved from Balakati Branch by 16 July and report at the Sambalpur Branch on 25 July.

I was relieved ceremoniously from the Balakati Branch. Departures are nothing but a stepping stone to a new beginning. I had wanted to make good use of the transition period between my joining dates, so I planned to visit Shirdi before joining at Sambalpur. I wanted to find my strength and anchor before taking up the transfer and receive Baba's blessings for ensuring a good all-round performance at Sambalpur as well. My husband and I booked train tickets for 17 July via Tatkal and travelled to Shirdi. We reached on the morning of 19 July. After a quick shower we went to the temple for a darshan. It was yet again a satisfying experience. The feeling of touching Shirdi soil is something different. But the real surprise was awaiting in my hotel room.

I had left my cellphone in my hotel room before going to the temple. After coming back when I glanced at my phone, I was shocked to see so many texts and missed calls. My first thought was whether Guddu and Chintu were all right. The phone rang again and broke my chain of thoughts, but catapulted me to cloud nine. The caller informed me of my selection as a CBS Faculty at the RTC, Bhubaneswar and my reporting date was on 1 August. It was an achievement because I was the first Odia lady officer to be selected as a Faculty in our Bhubaneswar Training college. I wanted to let out a shout of joy and happiness, but my moistened eyes did all the talking while I closed my eyes to thank Baba, the Director of this story, for such a happy ending.

When I started reviewing the chain of events, mere coincidences didn't explain what had happened. In this world of cut-throat competition, it was a lady colleague, who had applied for the same post, who informed me about the extension of date for submission of applications. She didn't have my contact number, so she must have made quite an effort to find it. Then, in the interview, I used PowerPoint for presentation for the first time ever yet, surprisingly, excelled in it. In short, when nothing was in my favour, there was the generous hand of my Baba over my head, who helped me to overcome the obstacles. Finally, light appeared at the end of the tunnel, shining in the form of Baba's face.

41

Ring a Bell

'But Mom nothing is fine. Why me? Why always me? Why doesn't anything fall in place for me smoothly at the first go? I'll put down my papers if I do not get what I want.'

His words left me completely speechless and I didn't have an answer to his grief and despair. My heart was breaking listening to my boy, but my mind wasn't ready to accept that this was the same boy who had always come on top after his duels with adversity.

A mother's happiness lies in the smile of her children and nothing wrings her heart more than their tears and sorrows. Inspired by my father who was in the Indian Air Force, my elder son, Koushik or Guddu, had decided to join the defence forces early in his life. He had gone to the Rashtriya Indian Military College, Dehradun, for his schooling followed by National Defence Academy, Pune, for his graduation. He had opted for the Naval wing and joined Naval Base at Kochi, from where he was commissioned into the Indian Navy in 2007.

Being a naval officer, sailing was an integral part of the job. Guddu had previously been on sailing trips abroad many times during his training. Everything was going well until 2010, when he started getting sea-sick. He had nausea and dizziness, sometimes accompanied by vomiting, due to the rocking or swaying motion of the vessel. The severity of his condition increased rapidly. He was in such a bad shape that blood would ooze out from his nose, besides vomiting, while on board. As a result, a strong aversion towards sailing started developing gradually within him. His physical condition started affecting his mental state. He used to share with me his troubles and hardships, but as a mother I could only try keeping his spirits high. I tried trivializing the matter by saying it was a generic condition which happened to all who were with him at sea. He wasn't convinced. He was keen on a base posting because his body resisted what his mind wanted. I couldn't accept this version of him because he has been an avid sportsman all his life, wining laurels after laurels as a matter of routine. Imagining him in this physically poor state made me very sad. Adding to this was my transfer to Sambalpur Branch on account of my promotion as Senior Manager. It wasn't the July monsoons that brought in the rain. These were indeed rainy days for our entire family.

At this point of time, I could have done anything I was asked to and resort to any sort of means to pull Guddu out of the extreme distress that he was in. Even though I do not believe in astrology, I met an astrologer just for my mental satisfaction. The astrologer's opinion was the usual – the fault was in his stars. He said that current time wasn't favourable for Guddu. (On reading this, Guddu will just laugh and ask, 'Mom, please tell me when has the time been favourable for me?'). The astrologer suggested wearing a ring with a stone matching his horoscope. I didn't agree and said I would discuss it with my husband. While on the way back, my mind was full of doubts. Should I go for the ring? Will it actually work? What if it doesn't? Why should I go for it when I leave everything to Baba?

Upon reaching home I spoke to my husband who concurred with what the astrologer had suggested.

Ring a Bell

Somehow, that's not what I wanted to hear from him. I just wasn't convinced. But I had to do something lest things went spiralling down further. I decided to have faith in my Master. I had believed in Him all this while, and everything had been good. So why not continue, then? Why have doubts over His powers? I realized I do not need to resort to a suggestion by an unknown astrologer when I had my own constant, proven Baba. I made up my mind. Sai Baba it would be for ever! The decision to choose Baba over the astrologer was solely mine.

While all this was going on, I got a call from Guddu stating that he had been admitted to the hospital at INS Ashwini, Mumbai, due to high fever and vomiting immediately on joining at Mumbai. His words wrung the soul out of me. At that point, the mother in me would have teleported herself to be alongside her son. But I controlled my emotions and asked him calmly if we could come and visit him. That was the intervening period between my being relieved from Balakati Branch on 16 July and before joining at Sambalpur on 25 July. I had earlier planned to travel to Shirdi during this period. Thus, it would be relatively easy for me to travel from Shirdi to Mumbai to meet Guddu. Anyway, his reply didn't conform to his usual behaviour and jolliness. His reply indicated that he wasn't in a good shape both physically and mentally. He said there was no point in coming. He was too sick to go out of the hospital to meet us and we would not be allowed inside the hospital due to high security protocols. So I dropped my plan of meeting Guddu during that trip.

But there was a sudden change. On the day of my journey to Shirdi, Guddu called to say that he would be happy to see us and we can visit him at the hospital. His tone sounded more positive than earlier. I was relieved to see the usual, happy-go-lucky and jovial side of my son coming back. I rescheduled the tickets so that we could travel from Shirdi to Mumbai and then back to Bhubaneswar.

Upon reaching Shirdi we had our first darshan of the day. As always, it was as pleasant as the first experience and every other darshan I had. In fact, every darshan brings along with it a new set of experiences. After coming out of the main hall, I decided to take the recommendation of the astrologer, but with a modification. I would get a ring for Guddu from Shirdi, with Baba's blessings. In the shop, I selected a ring which had Baba's face on it. There was an undefinable radiance to it. Baba's face exuded a comforting lustre which conveyed to me, 'There is nothing to fear my child. I'm still here.' On my next visit to the Samadhi Mandir, I gave the ring to the priest to get it blessed by Baba. He touched the ring to Baba's idol and lotus feet while reciting some mantras. I was observing all this, with my hands clasped and praying for Guddu's well-being. I had humbly requested Baba to give Guddu whatever he desired that would keep him happy and contented. Once the priest handed back the ring and other offerings, we left the Samadhi Mandir. All this time, my prayers to Baba were for So, Guddu's happiness. I just didn't want to see my son in a bad shape at any point of time.

We left for Mumbai after a couple of days at Shirdi. Guddu had made the arrangements for us to meet him through one of his friends. His friend received us at the station and took us inside the hospital after completing necessary security formalities.

Guddu had been steadily recovering at the hospital. Though he wasn't the usual self, bubbling with energy and high spirited, he looked healthy. But the moment he saw us, his bottled-up grief and despair burst out. He said, 'I'm not up for sailing. In fact, with this sea-sickness, I just won't be able to continue any further. No one is understanding the real problem that I'm facing. I'm the one out there on that vessel and not you. I know what it takes to be out there. Leave it! I just need a base posting.'

Ring a Bell

I didn't have any words to give him comfort or an acceptable solution. To console him, the moment I said, 'Guddu, listen, everything will be fine . . .', he had a complete breakdown. He said, 'But Mom nothing is fine, Why me? Why always me? Why doesn't anything fall in place for me smoothly at the first go? I'll put down my papers if I do not get what I want.'

His words left me completely speechless. I didn't have any answer to his grief and despair. My heart broke into pieces looking at him and listening to his words, but my mind wasn't ready to accept the situation.

My husband had been silent all this while. He is a man of few words, but he did speak at that moment. He assured Guddu that no matter what happened or what he decided to do, we would be there for him, always. This brought in a sense of peace and calmness to the tense atmosphere. I was still feeling helpless trying to find a method by which Guddu's issue could be solved.

Then an idea came to me. I requested Guddu to go outside the room and see the hospital premises. I said I would love to be at Ashwini just to enjoy the beautiful ambience. The three of us came out and sat in the beautiful lawn inside the hospital campus. I wanted to give the ring to Guddu. So I told him softly, 'Guddu, I have got you something and I want you to use it. Even if you don't feel like it, don't throw it away. Please keep it with you.' He was visibly shaken after hearing this and replied, 'Mom, have I ever thrown anything that you gave me? Remember, the Ganeshji idol and Sai Baba idol that you had given me when I was leaving for RIMC? I still have it after a decade or so. Why did you say something like this?' I immediately took out the ring from my bag and put it on his finger. The size was just right for him. It seemed it had been customized for him. Perhaps it was a subtle sign of the upcoming times.

Both my husband and I, watching the boy closely, the touch of that ring on his skin immediately brought about a visible change. It might sound like a scene from a movie, but it is the truth. The change was so clear and immediate that I was taken aback. His body language and reactions became closer to the original, lively boy, the one we knew all these years – the happy-go-lucky, jovial and cheerful Guddu. His charming smile returned on his face. With that his familiar love and care for us became obvious. He was worried that he was unable to ensure our comfort and a good stay due to his hospitalization.

I too started feeling better when he regained his composure and got back to his old self. He was relaxed and in a friendly mood started telling us stories about his lifestyle, friends and funny anecdotes about his friends. He told us that many of his friends who were posted in Mumbai visited him and were shocked to see a strong and fit character like him in that state. A sense of satisfaction was growing in me seeing Guddu the way he was then, all enthusiastic and cheerful. After a couple of hours, we left him at Ashwini and moved to the guest house in the Naval Base, accompanied by Guddu's friend. We stayed there for the night before leaving for Bhubaneswar the next day.

On the morning of 25th July I went to join office at the Sambalpur Zonal Office, though my posting was now limited to only seven days as I had to join as CBS Faculty at the Regional Training Centre, Bhubaneswar, from 1 August. In the evening, Guddu called me. Thankfully, he was sounding like his usual, old self. It was a great relief for me. Then I heard the whole story from him.

After our visit, the examining doctors had visited him. They enquired the reason of his stay when he had almost no fever. Guddu told them his problem of sea-sickness. The doctors patiently heard him out, and then asked him, 'What kind of assistance do you need from the medical team?'

Ring a Bell

While I was listening to what he said, what soothed my soul was that he was back to his normal self and sounded happy. I didn't say anything except asking him to take care of himself and to always share his situation with us. My parting words did not mention the actual reason behind the miraculous reversal and recovery process.

Guddu went through detailed medical tests. His problem of sea-sickness was categorized as 'high' and he was recommended for a base posting. He finally got his preferred base posting in October after having spent nearly four months in the hospital.

But the miraculous journey did not end there. Guddu chose the Provost branch which is the policing unit and looks after the safety and security of an entire Naval Base. For a specialized training course in Provost affairs, he was posted at Goa. He successfully completed the course and also topped it. He was given a cash prize of ☐25,000 as a merit scholarship. Someone correctly said, all is well that ends well.

Recently, when Guddu came home for his vacations, we were talking about this phase of his life. He said, 'I'm wondering what would have happened had you not visited. Thank you for coming over.' I instantly replied, 'Remember the ring I gave you? It had Baba's face on it. Now does that ring a bell?' His smile was the proof of my Baba's magic.

Looking back now, I think the ₹20 ring with Baba on it was better than that ring with a stone that was the astrologer's suggestion, which cost ₹7,000. Was the difference limited only to the price? Certainly not! The difference was between being persuaded blindly and pursuing a blind faith. I resorted to the latter and received Baba's blessings, as always.

The First Invitee and the Last in Attendance

In Odisha, it is a practice to invite Shri Jagannath of Puri first, before sending marriage invitation cards to friends and family. When my elder son Guddu's marriage was fixed, I had a wish of sending the marriage invitation to Shirdi Sai Baba as well.

Guddu's engagement ceremony was fixed for 19 February, and marriage on 2 May 2014. As we stay at Bhubaneswar, sending the first invitation to Lord Jagannath was easy. But the problem was to send the invitation to Sai Baba at Shirdi. Just then I remembered that there was a branch of UCO Bank at Shirdi. Each time I visited Shirdi, I also visited the Shirdi Branch. I contacted the Branch Manager whom I knew personally and requested help. He readily agreed. Along with the invitation card, I sent him a few essentials required for the rituals at Shirdi, along with a token amount of ₹101. The Branch Manager performed all the rituals on my behalf, deposited the offerings at the temple office and sent me the receipt. I was happy that this wish of mine was accomplished smoothly. I thanked Baba for accepting my invitation, sought His blessings for the wedding to be solemnized smoothly and requested His appearance for blessing us.

The First Invitee and the Last in Attendance

On the day of Guddu's engagement, while we were en route to the Surya Temple at Puri, the most welcoming and pleasant signs were awaiting us. We got down at Bata Mangala, a temple dedicated to the Goddess Mangala, to pay our obeisance. That very moment I saw a large sized calendar with Baba's image hanging on the wall. I immediately lit a diya, placed it before Baba and bowed before Him. This was followed by another sighting of Baba two days later, on 21 February when Guddu's ring ceremony was planned at Mayfair Lagoon, Bhubaneswar. We reached the venue much before the mahurat time and proceeded to the Convention Hall, where our function was scheduled. Just before entering the venue, at the entrance, I saw a beautiful idol of Baba, clad in a magnificent yellow dress. My happiness had no limit when I saw Him before my son and daughter-in-law exchanged their rings.

With Baba's blessings Guddu's marriage was solemnized with Luis, my daughter-in-law, on 2 May, in a most pleasant and enjoyable function. Baba's presence reiterated His Omnipresence, Omnipotence and Omniscience.

We had arranged the reception on 4 May at Rail Kunj, in an open area and not in the enclosed hall. In the late afternoon, black clouds started hovering in the sky and it started raining, with strong winds. My husband reached the venue to make alternate arrangements. Both my husband's and my phones were ringing continuously with queries from friends and relatives as to what would happen to the reception function. When my brother called about the arrangements, without hesitation I said Baba would take care of the situation and I had already invited Him.

The time for the reception in the invitation cards was 7.30 p.m., but we didn't expect guests to arrive before 8 p.m. By 8 p.m., the rain had completely stopped. And the rain was actually a blessing from Baba. It left behind a cool and pleasant atmosphere in the scorching heat of May. Our guests enjoyed themselves and blessed the newly-wedded couple. Their satisfaction and enjoyment were confirmed by the endless streams of calls and text messages I received the next day. On 1 May, during the pre-marriage rituals, I had lit an Akhand Jyoti diya before Baba, requesting Him to be with us all the time, and the diya was still burning on 5 May.

Although everything went so well, I still had a sense of incompleteness and a little disappointment because I hadn't seen Baba on the day of the reception.

On the fourth day after the marriage, there was a Havan at our home. The hectic marriage preparations had left me totally exhausted. I was lying down to give myself some rest but the non-sighting of Baba made me restless. The Havan got over and the couple started seeking blessings from the senior members of the family when I heard some people knocking at the door. I could also hear their voice calling out loudly, 'Maa'. Without informing anyone, I rushed downstairs to see an unbelievable sight. There were three men of different ages clad in Baba-like attire. I offered them seats and served them refreshments. I touched their feet for their blessings and gave them Dakshina. They happily accepted it and blessed me in their Hindi dialect.

When they left, all the family members enquired about my sudden absence. My happiness and satisfaction reflected in my reply. It was the perfect ending to one of the most beautiful new beginnings of my family. Clearly, it wasn't possible that Baba would forget this poor soul, come what may. Well, they have rightly said, save the best for the last, because the first invitee was last in attendance.

43

Loop of Devotion

On 19 October 2013 my husband and I were in Kathmandu, attending a Rotary conference with fellow Rotarians and their respective families. After the conference we were busy sightseeing in and around Pokhara. We went to Pashupatinath temple where we performed a ritual according to the traditions prevalent there and spent some time in the precincts of the temple. Somewhere at the back of my mind, I was searching for Baba's presence there as well. While walking around the temple complex I saw a photo of Baba placed at Jagyan Mandap, amongst other deities. All of a sudden, the trip felt complete and I felt elated after sighting Him.

Our return to Bhubaneswar was via Delhi, with a two-day stay at Delhi so that we could meet Chintu, my younger son, who had been working there for the previous few months. It was his first job after graduating from law school. We checked into the CRPF guest house at Nehru Nagar on 23 October and waited for Chintu to come over after his office.

In the evening, Chintu joined us at the guest house. We had a pleasant family time until the next morning when he left for his office. Given the fact that it was a Thursday, after Chintu left, I was restless to see Baba. I had made a habit of attending the Palki Yatra at Tankapani Road temple every Thursday, without fail. That habit motivated me to look for Baba. I decided to go out and have tea in some roadside stall. My husband agreed to accompany me and we walked out of the guest house. I recalled that I had read in some magazines that there was a Sai Baba temple at Lodhi Road. Out of sheer inquisitiveness, I enquired about it from a nearby auto driver. He said that the temple was nearby and he would take us there for only Rs 60. I changed my mind about having tea and decided to visit the temple instead. My husband couldn't understand the sudden change of plans but was more than happy to accompany me to the temple. The auto driver told us to expect a crowd as it was a Thursday, but I had no problem about it. We had a nice darshan and also had the delicious prasad.

Upon returning to the guest house, I thought I should make the most of my stay. I recalled there was a Sai Baba temple in Gurgaon called Sai ka Aangan and decided to visit it in the evening. I called Chintu and asked him to find the route and also accompany us for the visit.

In the evening, the three of us took a cab to Sai ka Aangan. Luckily, we got an opportunity to participate in the evening Aarti and the much talked-about Palki Yatra. The Palki Yatra was a very disciplined affair there because religious fervour was maintained along with proper rules and procedures. Most importantly, Baba looked adorable in an amazingly decorated Palki. The time well spent, we returned back contented.

The following day we had our return flight scheduled at 4 p.m. so there was time on our hands before we left for the airport. Without any second thoughts, my husband and I had headed to the Lodhi Road temple after breakfast. It was a Friday so the crowd was thinner than the previous day. We performed our rituals, gave our offerings, sat inside the temple and spent some time quietly in the lap of Baba. The experience was undoubtedly satisfying and as pleasant as the first experience at Tankapani Road.

It's that relentless wish to see Baba everywhere I go which makes me feel happy that I'm forever in the loop of His endless Devotion.

44

A New Beginning

Baba's miracles are unending. He transcends geographical limitations with His seamless omnipresence. Each time I start writing or sharing, the ink of my pen finishes, words fall short, papers get over, but Baba's leelas are an unending phenomenon. Therefore, all the small yet substantial miracles which didn't find an elaborate place earlier in this book are included in the following list:

- Visualizing Baba thrice in my dreams as if He was there to call me to complete some undone tasks was a once-in-a-lifetime experience.

- Though a common sight for me at my place, yet something worth mentioning – Each time I light a diya before Baba and pour my heart out to Him, the diya keeps burning until late evening and at times until midnight. The amount of ghee I put in is always the same, irrespective of the occasion.

- My posting at Balakati Branch was the best professional opportunity for me till today. Firstly, I was handed over the charge of a branch in the capacity of a Branch Manager. Secondly, Sai Baba Temple at Tankapani Road was on my route to office. So, I made it a point to call on Baba twice a day and at times thrice as well. The icing on the cake was that as a Branch Manager, I was successful in steering the branch to the top and we achieved all the parameters and completed all the targets. As a result of such exemplary performance, all my staff and I were given a certificate of appreciation along with cash prizes. It's pertinent to elaborate on the 'exemplary' part because our success story was published in SLBC news and our seniors used to quote this to other branches as a standard of performance and achievement. Whatever was done, was guided by an unseen hand.

- I remember, one day I was caught in a problematic situation and was just gazing at Baba's photo hanging on the wall. The gravity of the problem had rendered me helpless and out of the blue I had a call on my desk phone. When I answered the call it was the Zonal manager, who all by himself asked me, 'Do you need any assistance from Zonal office?' I was left speechless for a moment because I couldn't fathom whose voice it was – Zonal Manager or Baba. Needless to add, the problem was resolved.

- In March 2010 I had taken half-a-day off from work for the purchase of a new car. I had informed my staff about it but when the Zonal Manager called me and enquired about my whereabouts, I couldn't help but lie to him that I was out for deposit mobilization. The guilt of this lie diluted the happiness of owning a new car. Just when the pangs of this guilt were overpowering my conscience, I got a call from an unknown number. The person introduced himself and asked whether I would be present in office the next day. When I asked him the reason for his enquiry, he said that he wanted to deposit a cheque. The subsequent day he sent a cheque of ₹25 lakh to be deposited in a current account which had been

A New Beginning

inoperative since long. The chain of events didn't make sense to me unless I looked at it from the perspective of Baba. He changed my lie into a fact so that the residue of the earlier day was happiness and not guilt.

- Each time I desired to call on Him at Shirdi, the trip happened without fail, irrespective of how grim the situation was or slim were the chances.

- Last but never the least, upon my transfer to Delhi on deputation, I had many questions whether I'd be able to settle down and discharge my duties perfectly. Serendipity followed me when I saw Baba atop my desk on the first day of my joining the office. Furthermore, my area of work being limited to Service Tax and Income tax, I had to frequent those offices which were near Sai Baba Mandir at Lodhi Road and so I could visit Baba frequently.

Desires and wishes without expectations of returns always tend to be fulfilled. The ingredient to make this happen is a clear and pure heart submerged in the holy belief in Baba and devotion. Don't ask for easy and quick returns – with patience (Saburi) what you get will be more than expectations. Baba's arrival in my life came with a message to spread the idea of His devotion and miracles through my experiences. *Sai Musings* is a testament to it. His experiences are not just experienced but also re-lived during times when the going gets tough and hope is the only light at the end of the tunnel.

Nonetheless, I don't find the perfect conclusion to this book because *it is never the end, instead, it is a new beginning*!